ESTATE PUBLICATIONS

ALDERSHOT · CAMBERLEY
FARNBOROUGH · FARNHAM · FLEET

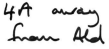

4A away
from Ald

G000111985

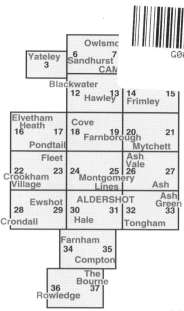

| Owlsmo |
| Yateley 6 7 Sandhurst |
| 3 CAM |
| Blackwater |
| 12 13 14 15 |
| Hawley Frimley |
| Elvetham Heath Cove |
| 16 17 18 19 20 21 |
| Pondtail Farnborough Mytchett |
| Fleet Ash Vale |
| 22 23 24 25 26 27 |
| Crookham Montgomery |
| Village Lines Ash |
| Ewshot ALDERSHOT Ash Green |
| 28 29 30 31 32 33 |
| Crondall Hale Tongham |
| Farnham |
| 34 35 |
| Compton |
| The Bourne |
| 36 37 |
| Rowledge |

| ROAD MAP | Page 2 |
| INDEX TO STREETS | Page 38 |

Scale of street plans: 4 Inches to 1 Mile (unless otherwise stated)

Motorway	Stream / River
'A' Road / Dual	Canal
'B' Road / Dual	→ One-way Street
Minor Road / Dual	🅿 Car Park
Track	🄲 Public Convenience
Pedestrianized	🄸 Tourist Information
Railway / Station	✚ Place of Worship
Footpath	● Post Office

Every effort has been made to verify the accuracy of information in this book but the publishers cannot accept responsibility for expense or loss caused by an error or omission. Information that will be of assistance to the user of the maps will be welcomed.

The representation on these maps of a road, track or path is no evidence of the existence of a right of way.

Street plans prepared and published by ESTATE PUBLICATIONS, Bridewell House, TENTERDEN, KENT.
The Publishers acknowledge the co-operation of the local authorities
of towns represented in this atlas.

Ordnance Survey® This product includes mapping data licensed from Ordnance Survey® with the permission of the Controller of Her Majesty's Stationery Office.

Bagshot

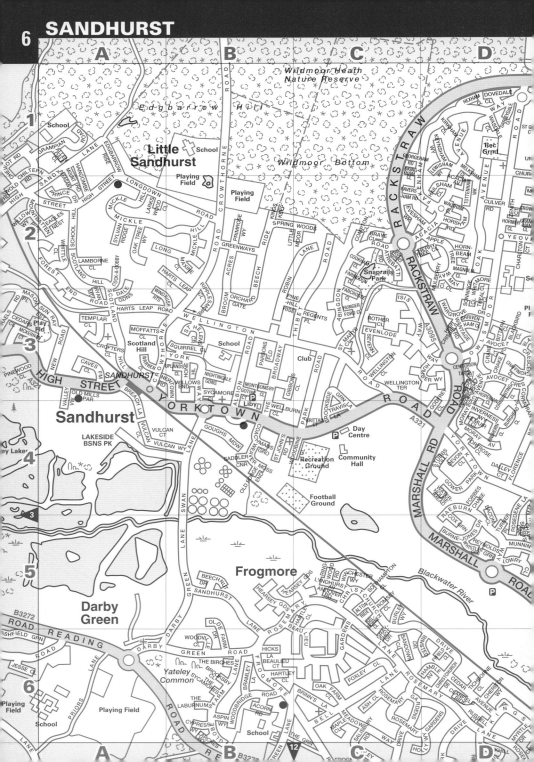

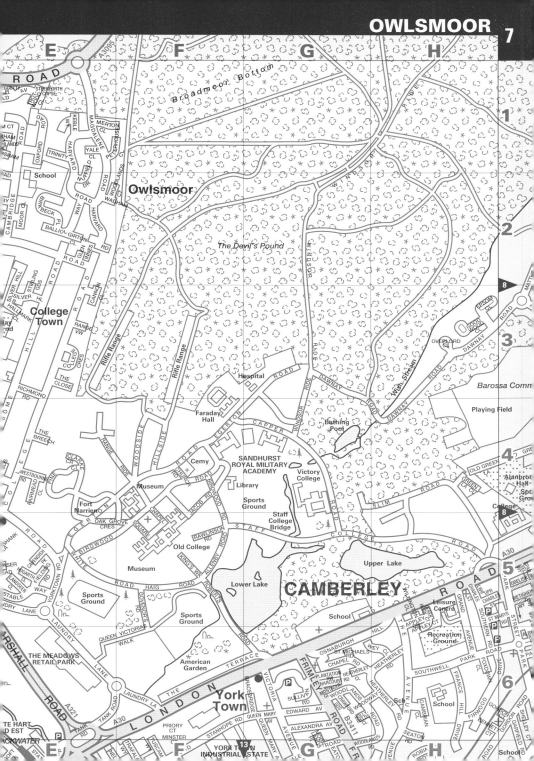

E F G H

ROAD
A3095

Broadmoor Bottom

1

STEERFORTH COPSE
GOODY DL
AV

M CT
HAM
HLANDS
CT
SHAM

OXFORD
KEBLE
HARVARD
MAGDALENE
MERTON
PETERHOUSE
YALE CL

School

TRINITY
BECK PL
GIRTON RD
GLEN INNES RD
BALLIOL CL

Owlsmoor

WADHAM

Owlsmoor

HARVARD ROAD

2

The Devil's Pound

CAMBRIDGE ROAD
SILVER HILL
STIRLING GDNS
HALLMARK
MOOR CL
CANNON
GLEN INNES RD
RANGE VW

WINDSOR RIDE

College
Town

RANGE ROAD
CLLEGI CRES
Rifle Range
Rifle Range

8

EPSOM
OVERLORD RD
GOOD WOOD CL
DAWNAY

3

RICHMOND RD
THE CLOSE

Hospital

ROAD

Barossa Comn

WISH-STREAM

DAWNAY ROAD

Playing Field

THE BREECH

Faraday
Hall

EGERTON ROAD
CAPPER

DAWNAY ROAD
WINDSOR RIDE

4

CLARE CFT
CLMc
FERNE RD
WESTBOURNE RD
HARMEAD RD

WOODSIDE
HILLSIDE

Cemy

SANDHURST
ROYAL MILITARY
ACADEMY

Bathing
Pool

OLD GREEN LA
GREEN LA CL

Alanbrot
Hall
Spt
Gro

Museum

BRICK HILL
JACOB RD
BIRDWOOD RD
RAWLINSON RD

Library

Victory
College

SLIM ROAD

COLLEGE ROAD

8

Fort
Narrien

CHAPEL SQUARE
OAK GROVE CRES
ALLENBY RD
STAFF RD

Sports
Ground

Staff
College
Bridge

College

EGERTON ROAD
WHITE ROAD
BIRDWOOD ROAD

Old College

A30 ROAD

5

SHANK
CAERLEON RD
HOGARTH RD
FIELDING WAY
LANDSER RD
STABLE
NDRY LANE

YORKTOWN ROAD

Museum

KING'S WK
HAIG ROAD
ROBERTS ROAD

Lower Lake

Upper Lake

CAMBERLEY

Leisure
Centre

OBELISK
CHARLES ST MARYS RD
UPR CHARLES
GRAND AV
SOUTHERN

BIETGHER

Sports
Ground

GOVENOR'S RD

Sports
Ground

School

Recreation
Ground

APPLEY CT
APPLEY RD
ST MARYS RD

PARK AVENUE

6

THE MEADOWS
RETAIL PARK

LAUNDRY LANE

QUEEN VICTORIA WALK

American
Garden

THE TERRACE

FRIMLEY ROAD

OSNABURGH
ST MICHAELS
CHAPEL RD

WEY LA
HEATHERLEY
HEATHERLEY CL

SOUTHWELL
PARK
FRANCE HILL DRIVE

School

GORDON RD
SHELLEY RD
GARFIELD RD

TE HART
D EST
CKWATER

A321 ROAD
LONDON ROAD
A30

TANK RD
TUSCANI
TRAFALGAR

PRIORY CT
MINSTER

York
Town

BRACEBRIDGE
VICTORIA

SULLIVAN
EDWARD AV
STANHOPE RD
QUEEN MARY
ALEXANDRA AV

PLANTATION
HARCOURT RD
MONTAGUE
WOODLANDS
CHWN WK
WOODWAY RD

HEATHERLEY RD

SEATON RD
WOODLANDS

CAMBRIAN CL
BENNET RD

FIRWOOD DR
ROBIN

School

13
YORK TOWN
INDUSTRIAL ESTATE

E F G H

School

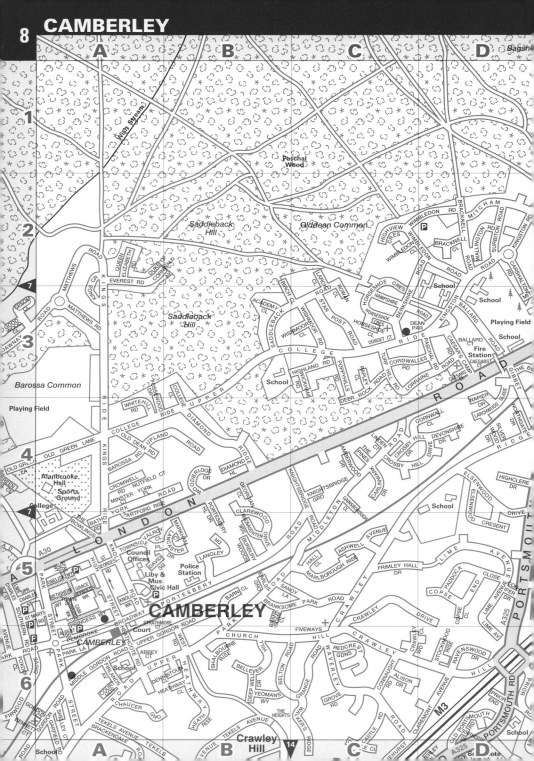

A · **B** · **C** · **D**

Pont Hill

BLACKBUSHES ROAD

Lichett Plain

Word Hill Farm

TURNERS GRN LANE

Sewage Works

Doghouse Bridge

Doghouse Copse

Gilldown Farm

Elvetham · **Rotten Green**

STREET END

A323

M3 P

FLEET SERVICES P

Elvetham Heath

LYNDHURST
ROTHERWICK HO
OAKHANGER HO
KINGSLEY SQ
KINGS/LEY
KINGSWORTHY RD

OVINGTON DR
MATTINGLEY WAY
HECKFIELD DR
HEADLEY MOUNTS
MICHELDEVER
FARLEIGH WALL
DR ELVEST
HAZELEY MOUNTS
FULLERTON DR

TADLEY
KENSINGTON CT
MAYFAIR
UPTON
TURNERS
WEST TISTED
UPTON GREY DR

WHITCHURCH RD

Temporary School

Community Centre

School

HEATH WAY

WAY

Palelane Farm

Parkfield Copse

Great Bog Copse

ELVETHAM ROAD

Park & Ride P

ELVETHAM

ELVETHAM PL

HOSPITAL

PHEASANT COPSE

CALTHORPE

Railroad Copse

GLENDALE PK

READING ROAD

CALTHORPE RD
BROOMRIGG RD
HAGLEY RD
GOUGH
CHURCH RD
GOUGH RD
CHURCH RD
SUNNYSIDE
PEAT MOOR
CHURCH RD
BRANKSOMEWOOD RD
ORCHARD
VICTORIA HILL RD
CHURCH GRO
VICTORIA RD

QUEEN MARY AVE

PINE

ROSEDEN GDS

Culver Copse

FITZROY
BELVEDERE DR
GLENDALE
PERRYS DR
DUKES DR
TAVISTOCK
THE OAKS
MEAD

BROOMRIGG RD

HERBERT ROAD

NORTH READING ROAD

THE AVENUE
A323
SPRINGFIELD LA

Fleet

Park

BRANKSOME CT

VICTORIA GDS
MDW CL
SOVEREIGN
CP

Hitches Farm

MONKS

A · **B** · **C** · **D**

22

E   F   G   H

1

2

3

4

5

6

18

18

23

Minley Woods

B3013

BCKBUSHES

MINLEY   ROAD

Mallards Copse

M3

Ancels Copse

Little Bramshot Farm

A3013

BARLEY WY   HARVEST   CRESCENT   RYE CL   ANCELLS CT

ANCELLS   ROAD   THE GATES

KERRY   RYELAND CL   WAY   COLERIDGE   FALLOW DR

DRIVE   SHETLAND   COWER   OASTHOUSE CNR   MILL DR

BACK WY   FARM   ANGORA   BEVERLEY   THRESHERS   DROVERS END

DRIVE   ARGENTE   CL   CHESTNUT   ROAD

DIBLE WY   FARM   SWALEDALE   GDS   CHERBERRY CL

TAMWORTH   FRIESIAN   CL   FAULKNERS

DEXTER   GUERNSEY   DRIVE   SUSSEX DR   HANOVER   FOREST

WY   DEVON   HIGHLAND   GALLOWAY   DEAN

MEAD   ANCELLS   SHIRE AVENUE

FOXWOOD   WOODGATE

Park

DRIVE

SANKEY LANE

Golf Course

COVE   ROAD   COVE   ROAD   COVE

CYGNET   COVE RD

CTDE   WATERSIDE   LAKESIDE

MINLEYS   CT   ATTENBROUGH

FLEET   P   GRO

STA APP

WATERFRONT BUSINESS PARK

ELVETHAM   ROAD

ELVETHAM   COACH HO   KNOLL   OWENSLEY   FLEET RD

CL   GDNS   KNOLL RD   CRANBROOK   DARSET AV

TAVERLEY   THE MOUNT   BRAMSHOT DR

Fleet Pond (Nature Reserve)

WAVERLEY   AV   KNOLL   HIGHDOWN   AVONDALE   HILL   WELLINGTON   CHESTNUT   GROVE   BROOKLY GDNS

SEYMOOR CT   PINEWOOD   DUNMOW   CL

AVENUE

KINGS   A3013   ROAD

FUGELMERE WK   KENT   FUGELMERE   RD

KENILWORTH   ROAD   END PUMP   HO CL

PK WESTMINSTER CL   BIRCH AV   ST PHILIPS CT   HILL   KENT

STREET   OLD SCH   SOUTHBY DR   KEVINS GRO   BERKELEY CL   HONISTER GDNS

WINCHESTER   BEARWOOD GDNS   THE LAURELS   WINDSOR CT   LESTOCK

CHURCH   CLARENCE   CONNAUGHT   ABBOTS CL   CRNSIDE   B3010   ROAD   COOMBE   ADAMS DR

CARNIVAL   VICTORIA CT   ROAD   Oakley Park   WOOD   LANE

COTSWOLD CT   GEOF   RD   ALBANY   KBATS GDS   WOOD ELMS   FRENSH AV

KENWORTH AV   GOLDFORD   CYPRESS   HERMES DR   CEDAR   CAMDEN   LYNDALE   ROWAN AV   SPRUCE

WOODSIDE GDNS

Calvert Stream

Pondtail

WEIR

ROXBEE

COVE

ROAD

KINGS   ROAD   FLEET   KINGS   ROAD

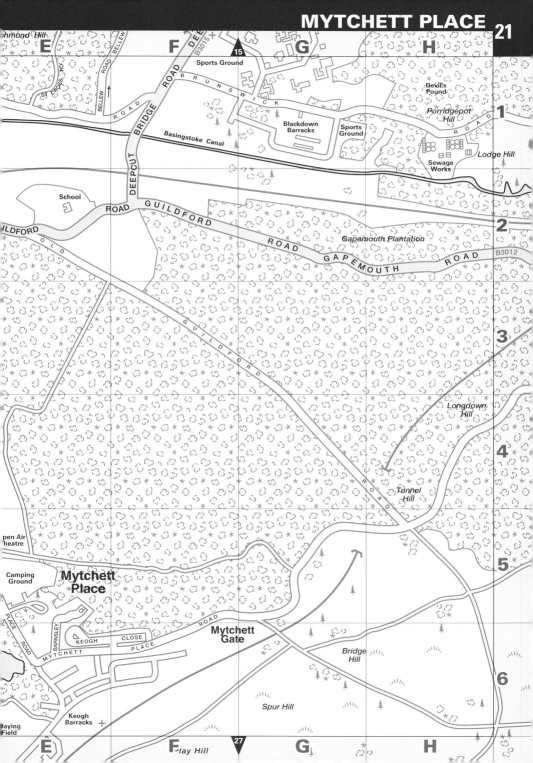

E   **F**   **G**   **H**

hmond Hill

B3015

Sports Ground

15

ST CROSS RD

ROAD BELLEW

BRIDGE ROAD

DEEP

BRUNSWICK

Devil's Pound

Porridgepot Hill

ROAD

ROAD

Basingstoke Canal

Blackdown Barracks

Sports Ground

Sewage Works

Lodge Hill

1

DEEPCUT

School

ROAD GUILDFORD ROAD

Gapemouth Plantation

GAPEMOUTH ROAD

B3012

ILDFORD

OLD

2

GUILDFORD

3

Longdown Hill

4

ROAD

Tunnel Hill

pen Air Theatre

5

Camping Ground

Mytchett Place

ROAD

Mytchett Gate

Bridge Hill

PLACE

CL

BARNSLEY

KEOGH

CLOSE

PLACE

MYTCHETT

ROAD

6

Keogh Barracks

Spur Hill

laying Field

E   **F**   **G**   **H**

27

lay Hill

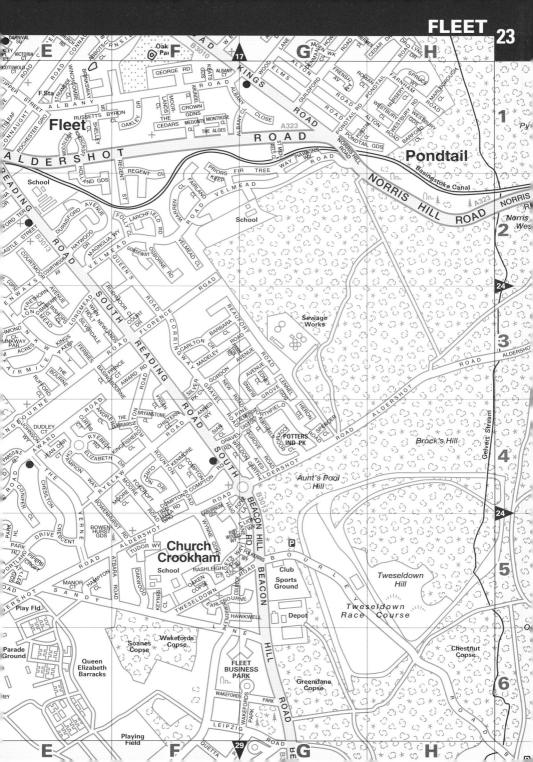

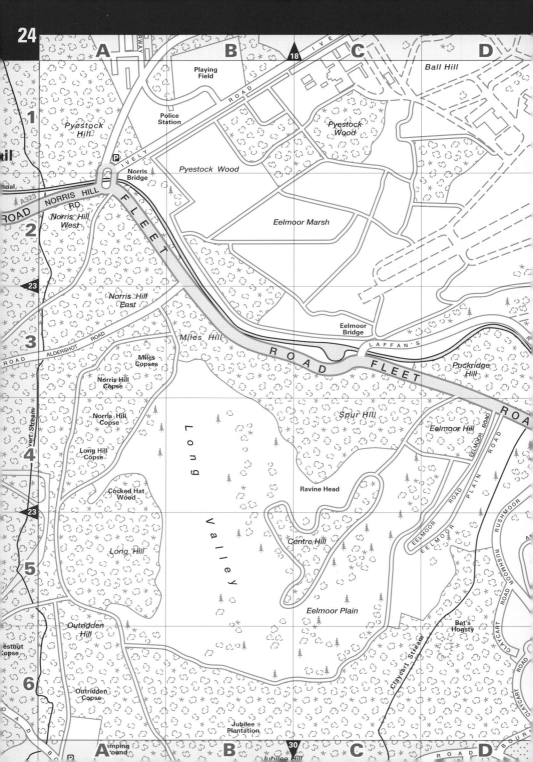

A **B** △18 **C** **D**

Ball Hill

Playing Field

Police Station

1

Pyestock Hill

Pyestock Wood

Pyestock Wood

ROAD

IVELY

P

Norris Bridge

Pyestock Wood

Canal

ROAD

A323

NORRIS HILL

RD

Eelmoor Marsh

2

Norris Hill West

FLEET

△23

Norris Hill East

Eelmoor Bridge

3

Miles Hill

LAFFAN'S

ROAD

FLEET

ROAD

ALDERSHOT ROAD

Miles Copses

Norris Hill Copse

Spur Hill

Puckridge Hill

Eelmoor Hill

Long

ert. Stream

Norris Hill Copse

Long Hill Copse

Valley

EELMOOR ROAD

RUSHMOOR

4

Ravine Head

EELMOOR ROAD

PLAIN ROAD

Cocked Hat Wood

△23

Centre Hill

EELMOOR ROAD

RUSHMOOR ROAD

5

Long Hill

Eelmoor Plain

Bat's Hogsty

CLAYCART ROAD

Outridden Hill

estnut opse

Claycart Stream

CLAYCART ROAD

6

Outridden Copse

BOUR

ROAD

Jubilee Plantation

A amping ound P **B** △30 **C** **D**

Jubilee Hill

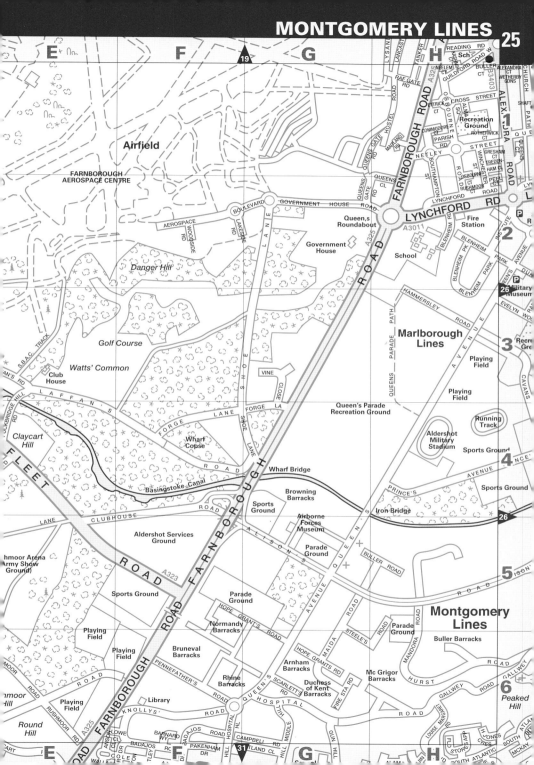

E   F   19   G   H   Sch   1

READING RD
LYSAN
LANCASTER
TANKER
GUILDFORD ROAD
NEELEM
RAF GATE
RD
ALEXANDRA
CT
WETHERBY
GDNS
CHURCH
B3403
SHAFT
CT
PATRICK
CROSS
STREET
CT
CT
COURSE
CT
ALMA
Recreation
Ground
ROTHERWICK
PARISH
ALEX.RA ROAD
QUE
1
Airfield
COMMODORE
SOUTHAMPTON
NETLEY
ST
STREET
GRESHAM
TREDEN
WINCHEM
HAM
DOSBURNE
RUSHMOOR
PEEL
QUEENS
LY
FARNBOROUGH
AEROSPACE CENTRE
HOSTEL
QUEENS
GATE
RD
QUEENS
GATE
CL
LYNCHFORD
ST
L

P
2
QUEENS
GATE
Fire
Station
LYNCHFORD RD
A3011

BOULEVARD
GOVERNMENT HOUSE ROAD
Queen,s
Roundabout
A325
BLENHEIM
BLENHEIM PK
BLENHEIM
PARK
AVENUE
WITE
AVENUE
P
D

AEROSPACE
WOODSIDE
RD
LAKESIDE
RD
LANE
Government
House
School
BLENHEIM
PARK
26
Military
Museum
QUE

Danger Hill
ROAD
HAMMERSLEY
PARADE
PATH
ROAD
AVENUE
26
Military
Museum
EVELYN
WO
Recr
Gr
3

Golf Course
VINE
QUEENS
Marlborough
Lines
Playing
Field
Playing
Field
CAVAN,S

Watts' Common
Club
House
SHOE
FORGE LA
CLOSE
Queen's Parade
Recreation Ground
Aldershot
Military
Stadium
Running
Track
Sports Ground
4
NCE

S.B.A.C. TRACK
AN'S RD
LAFFAN'S
FORGE
LANE
SHOE
LANE
PRINCE'S
AVENUE
Sports Ground
NCE

Claycart
Hill
CKBRIDGE HILL
ROAD
Basingstoke Canal
ROAD
Wharf
Copse
ROAD
Wharf Bridge
Browning
Barracks
Sports
Ground
Iron Bridge
26

FLEET
LANE
CLUBHOUSE
Aldershot Services
Ground
FARNBOROUGH
ALISON'S
Airborne
Forces
Museum
Parade
Ground
BULLER ROAD
QUEEN'S
ROAD
5
SON

hmoor Arena
Army Show
Ground)
ROAD
A323
Sports Ground
Parade
Ground
MAIDA
STEELE'S
Parade
Ground
Montgomery
Lines
Buller Barracks

Playing
Field
Playing
Field
Bruneval
Barracks
PENNEFATHER'S
Normandy
Barracks
HOPE GRANT'S ROAD
Rhine
Barracks
Arnham
Barracks
Duchess
of Kent
Barracks
HOPE GRANTS RD
FIRE STA RD
Mc Grigor
Barracks
MANDORA
HURST
ROAD
GALLWEY
ROAD
6
Peaked
Hill

MOOR
ROAD
RUSHMOOR RD
Playing
Field
Round
Hill
KNOLLYS'
Library
LOWE
ANSON
BADAJOS
BARNARD
WY
PAKENHAM
DR
31
TLAND CL
FARNBOROUGH
A325
ROAD
QUEEN'S
SCARLETT'S RD
HOSPITAL
HL
HILL
MIDDLE
HILL
CAMPBELL RD
LOUISE MARGI
JONES
ATLANTIC
SOUTH ATLANTIC
MCKAY

E   F   31   G   H

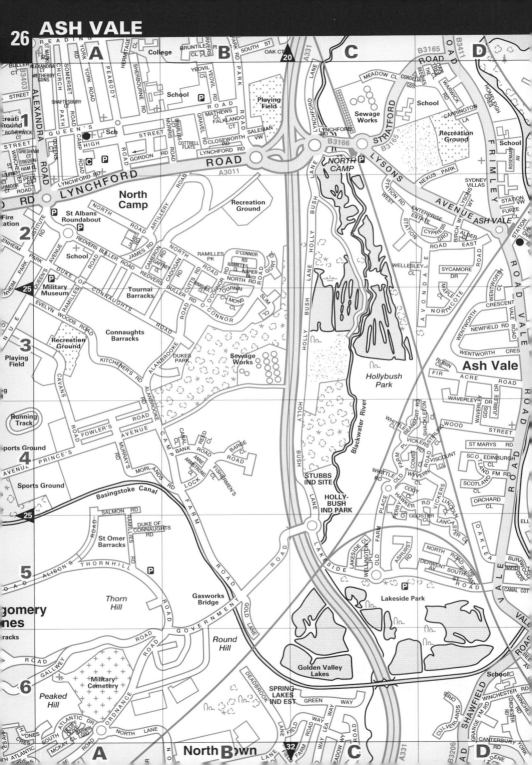

A — Hancock's Farm
B
22
C — WATERY LANE — DU MAURIER LANE
D

1
Coxmoor Farm
Oakes Copse
Leeches Copse
Five Acres Copse
Six Acre Copse
Bowenhurst Farm
Goose Close
Fusney Copse
Redfield Rows

Mill Lane

2
Golf Course
BOWENHURST
CRONDALL ROAD
REDFIELDS
FARNHAM ROAD A287
ROAD FARNHAM ROAD
DARE'S LANE
DARE'S LANE
Dare's Corner

BOWLING ALLEY
Downsland Copse
Little Down Copse
BOWLING ALLEY LANE
PANKRIDGE STREET
BOWLING ALLEY

3
Bowling Alley
Hannam's Copse
LEFROY'S FLD
HANDCROFT CL
GREEN SPRINGS
ASHLEY CL
STREET
REDLANDS
Withy Copse
LANE

4
HYDE
DITCHEL
HANNAM'S FRM CL
THE WITHES
THE JOLLIES
PANKRIDGE STREET
Golf Course
LANE
The Tileries

5
Crondall
LANE ROAD
THE BOROUGH
DIPPENHALL
CHURCH STREET
HILL YER
ORCHARD CT
LANE RD
GLEBE RD
ST CROSS
HEATH STREET
DIPPENHALL ROAD

6
WELL
CROFT LANE
CROFT
FARM LA
School
RAVELIN CL
CHAUNDLERS CROFT
STREET
Lawn

A
B
C
D

Playing Field

Leipzig Barracks

QUETTA

LEIPZIG

PARK

23

B3013

BEACON HILL ROAD

Beaconhill Copse

BOURLEY LANE

BOL

1

QUETTA PARK

Pankhurst Hill

Ridding's Copse

LANE

Beacon Hill Farm

Bourley Bottom

Reservoir

2

EWSHOT

LANE

Seymour Farm

Beacon Hill

30

LANE

TADPOLE

Recreation Ground

Hall

Abury Hill

LANE

CHURCH

Homecroft Farm

BEACON HILL ROAD

3

Skains Copse

HIGH

LANE

Turner's Copse

Bricksbury Hill

Combe Wood

WOODPECKER

BADGER

NIGHTJAR CL

PARTRIDGE CL

MAGPIE CL

ODIHAM

BROOMHILL

WAY

Ewshot

SPARROWHAWK

NUTHATCH

FOX

WAY

KESTREL CL

CL

4

Ewshot Wood

LANE

WARREN CORNER

EWSHOT HL

DORA'S GRN

CROSS LA

DORA'S GREEN LANE

Warren Corner

ODIHAM

ROAD

ODIHAM

ROAD

30

UP

FO

DLANDS

E A T H

A287

Lands Copse

Ewshot Farm

A3

A287

OLD

PARK

LANE

HEATHYFIELDS RD

OLD

PARK

CLOSE

5

The Warren

HEATHYFIELDS

ROAD

R OLD

Upper Old Park

6

DORA'S GREEN

Dora's Green

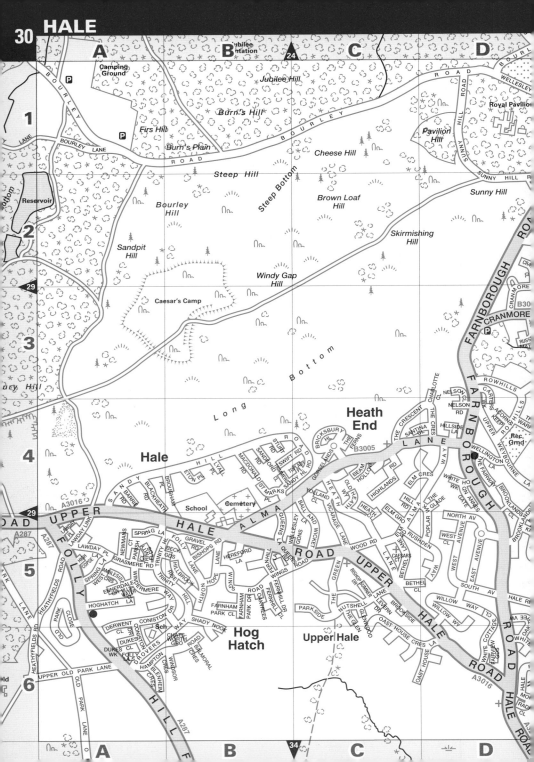

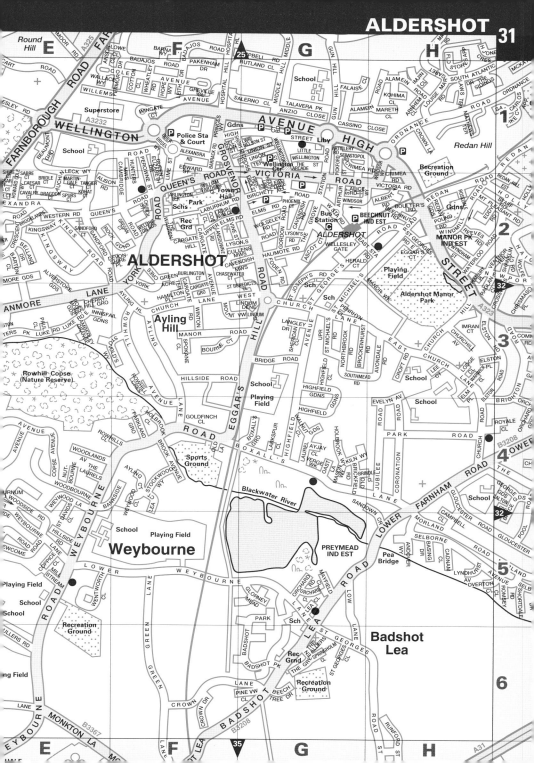

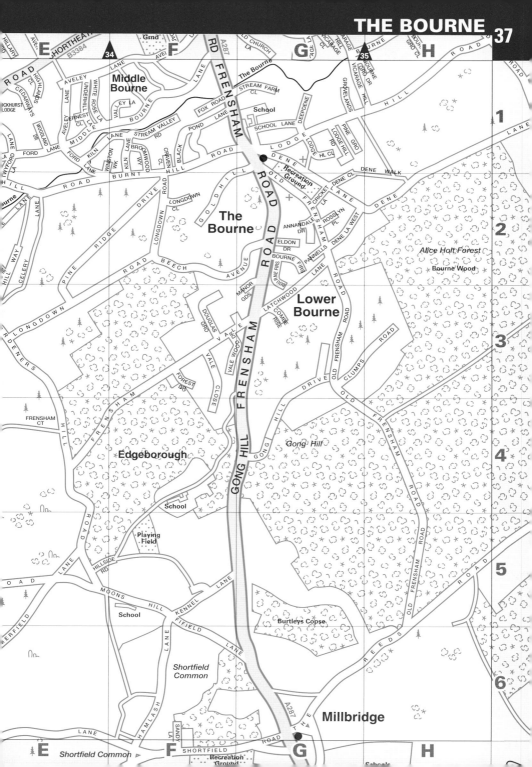

A - Z INDEX TO STREETS
with Postcodes

The Index includes some names for which there is insufficient space on the maps. These names are indicated by an * and are followed by the nearest adjoining thoroughfare.

Abbetts La GU15 13 H2
Abbey Ct, Camberley GU15 8 A6
Abbey Ct, Farnham GU9 34 D4
Abbey St GU9 34 D4
Abbey Way GU14 19 H3
Abbots CI GU51 17 E6
Abbots Ride GU9 35 F5
Abelia CI GU24 11 F5
Abingdon Rd GU47 6 C3
Acacia Av GU47 6 C2
Academy CI GU15 8 B3
Acheulian CI GU9 34 D6
Acorn Keep GU9 30 D4
Acorn Mws GU14 13 G6
Acorn Rd GU17 6 B6
Adams Dr GU51 17 G6
Adams Park Rd GU9 35 E2
Addison Rd GU16 14 C5
Adlington Pl GU14 20 B5
Admiralty Way GU15 13 E1
Aerospace Blvd GU14 25 F2
Ainger Ct GU12 32 A1
Aircraft Esp GU14 19 H6
Aisne Rd GU16 15 H4
Alamein Rd GU11 31 H2
Alanbrooke Rd GU11 26 A3
Albany CI GU51 23 F1
Albany Ct GU51 23 F1
Albany Pk GU16 13 H4
Albany Pk Ind Est GU16 13 H4
Albany Rd GU51 23 E1
Albert Rd, Aldershot GU11 31 H2
Albert Rd, Bagshot GU19 9 H2
Albert Rd, Camberley GU15 8 A6
Albert Rd, Farnborough GU14 19 H6
Albert St GU51 17 E6
Albion Rd GU47 6 B4
Alder CI GU12 26 D2
Alder Gro GU46 3 C3
Aldershot Rd, Aldershot GU12 32 C3
Aldershot Rd, Church Crookham GU52 23 E5
Aldershot Rd, Fleet GU52 22 D6
Aldrin Pl GU14 18 D4
Aldwick CI GU14 19 G1
Alexandra Av GU15 7 G6
Alexandra Ct GU14 25 H1
Alexandra Rd, Aldershot GU11 31 E2
Alexandra Rd, Aldershot GU11 31 F1
Alexandra Rd, Ash GU12 32 C2
Alexandra Rd, Farnborough GU14 19 H5
Alfonso CI GU12 32 A3
Alfred Rd GU9 34 D4
Alfriston Rd GU16 15 F6
Alice Rd GU11 31 G2
Alison CI GU14 19 F4
Alison Dr GU15 8 C6
Alison Rd GU11 31 E2
Alisons Rd GU11 25 G5
All Saints Cres GU14 13 E4
All Saints Rd GU18 10 C2
Allden Av GU12 32 A4
Allden Gdns GU12 32 A4
Allenby Rd GU15 7 F5
Allendale CI GU47 6 A1
Alma CI GU12 32 B1
Alma Gdns GU16 15 G5
Alma La GU9 30 B5
Alma Sq GU14 25 H1
Alma Way GU9 30 C5

Almond CI GU14 13 G6
Almond Ct GU52 23 G4
Almondale Ct GU14 19 G1
Alpha Rd GU12 32 B2
Alphington Av GU16 14 C4
Alphington Grn GU16 14 C4
Alpine CI GU14 18 D4
Alsace Walk GU15 13 H4
Alsford CI GU18 10 A4
Alton Rd, Farnham GU10 36 A1
Alton Rd, Fleet GU51 23 G1
Alton Ride GU17 6 C5
Alverstoke Gdns GU11 31 E2
Amber Hill GU15 15 F1
Amberley Grange GU11 31 E3
Amberwood Dr GU15 8 C4
Ambleside CI, Farnborough GU14 19 E4
Ambleside CI, Mytchett GU16 20 D5
Ambleside Cres GU9 30 A5
Ambleside Rd GU18 10 A3
Ancells CI GU51 17 G2
Ancells Rd GU51 17 F3
Anchor Mdw GU14 19 F4
Anderson Pl GU19 4 C4
Andover Dr GU51 16 B5
Andover Rd GU17 6 C5
Andover Way GU11 31 H5
Andrew Ct GU14 13 F5
Andrewartha Rd GU14 20 B6
Andrews CI GU52 23 E4
Andrews Rd GU14 19 E2
Angers CI GU15 9 F4
Anglesey Av GU14 13 F6
Anglesey Rd GU12 32 A2
Angora Way GU51 17 F3
Annandale Rd GU14 37 G2
Anne Armstrong CI GU11 26 B4
Annes Way GU52 23 F4
Annettes Cft GU52 22 D5
Ansell Rd GU16 14 B5
Anson CI GU11 31 E1
Anzio CI GU11 31 G1
Apex Dr GU16 14 B5
Aplin Way GU18 10 B3
Apollo Rise GU14 18 D4
Apple Tree Way GU47 6 D2
Appledore Mws GU14 13 F6
Applelands CI GU10 36 D3
Appley CI GU15 7 H6
Appley Dr GU15 7 H5
April CI GU15 13 H3
Aragon Rd GU46 3 C4
Ardrossan Av GU15 14 D1
Arena La GU11 24 D5
Argente CI GU51 17 F3
Arlington Ter GU11 31 F2
Armitage Dr GU16 14 D4
Armstrong Mall GU14 18 C3
Arnhem CI GU11 31 H1
Arrow Ind Est GU14 19 F5
Arrow Rd GU14 19 F5
Arthur CI, Bagshot GU19 9 H2
Arthur CI, Farnham GU9 34 C5
Arthur Rd GU9 34 C5
Arthur St GU11 31 G2
Artillery Rd, Aldershot GU11 31 G1
Artillery Rd, North Camp GU11 26 A2
Arundel CI GU51 23 F1
Arundel Pl*, The Hart GU9 34 C3
Arundel Rd GU15 15 F1
Ascot Ct GU11 31 G2
Ash Church Rd GU12 33 E2
Ash CI, Ash GU12 27 E6
Ash CI, Camberley GU17 6 C6
Ash Green La East GU12 33 F3
Ash Green La West GU12 32 C4
Ash Green Rd GU12 33 F3
Ash Hill Rd GU12 27 E6

Ash Lodge CI GU12 32 D2
Ash Lodge Dr GU12 32 C3
Ash Rd GU12 32 A3
Ash St GU12 32 C2
Ash Tree CI GU14 18 C4
Ashbourne CI GU12 27 F6
Ashbury Dr GU17 13 F4
Ashdene Cres GU12 32 D1
Ashdene Rd GU12 32 D1
Ashdown Av GU14 20 B5
Ashfield Grn GU46 3 F3
Ashley CI, Crondall GU10 28 B4
Ashley CI, Farnborough GU16 20 D1
Ashley Dr GU17 12 C1
Ashley Rd GU14 20 A4
Ashley Way GU24 11 E5
Ashridge GU14 13 E6
Ashurst Rd GU12 26 C5
Ashwell Av GU15 8 C5
Aspin Way GU17 6 B6
Atbara Rd GU12 23 F5
Atfield Gro GU20 5 G4
Atrebatti Rd GU47 6 C2
Attenborough CI GU51 17 G4
Attfield CI GU12 32 C2
Attlee Gdns GU52 23 E5
Auchinleck Way GU11 31 E2
Augustus Gdns GU15 9 F6
Austen Rd GU14 19 G1
Aveley La GU9 34 D6
Avenue Rd, Farnborough GU14 20 A3
Avenue Rd, Fleet GU51 16 D5
Avenue Sucy GU15 13 G1
Avery CI*, York Cres GU11 31 F2
Avocet Cres GU47 6 D3
Avon CI, Aldershot GU12 32 D3
Avon CI, Farnborough GU14 13 E6
Avon Ct GU9 34 D5
Avon Rd GU9 34 D5
Avondale GU12 26 D3
Avondale Rd, Aldershot GU11 31 H3
Avondale Rd, Fleet GU51 17 E5
Award Rd, Church Crookham GU52 22 D5
Award Rd, Church Crookham GU52 23 F3
Ayesgarth GU52 23 G4
Ayjay CI GU11 31 G4
Ayling CI GU9 31 F4
Ayling Hill GU11 31 F3
Ayling La GU11 31 F3
Ayrshire Gdns GU51 17 F4
Azalea Way GU15 9 E5

Babbs Mead GU9 34 B4
Bacon CI GU47 6 D4
Badajos Rd GU11 25 F6
Badger Dr GU18 10 A2
Badger Way GU10 29 F4
Badgers CI GU52 22 D2
Badgers Copse GU15 14 C2
Badgers Holt GU46 3 B4
Badgerwood Dr GU14 14 B3
Badshot Lea Rd GU9 31 F6
Badshot Pk GU9 31 G6
Bagshot Grn GU19 4 C6
Bagshot Rd GU24 11 E4
Baigents La GU20 5 G4
Bailey CI GU16 14 A5
Baileys CI GU17 12 B1
Bain Av GU15 13 G3
Baird Rd GU14 20 A1
Bakehouse Mws*, High St GU11 31 G1
Baldreys GU9 34 B6
Balintore Ct GU47 6 D3
Ball and Wicket La GU9 30 C4
Ballantyne Rd GU14 19 F1

Ballard Ct GU15 8 D3
Ballard Rd GU15 8 D3
Balliol Way GU47 7 E2
Balmoral Cres GU16 30 B6
Balmoral Dr GU16 14 C5
Balmoral Rd GU12 8 B5
Banbury CI GU16 14 D6
Banbury Woods GU15 8 B5
Bank Rd GU11 26 B4
Bankside GU9 31 E4
Bannister Gdns GU46 3 F3
Barbara CI GU12 23 F3
Barberry CI GU52 23 E3
Barberry Way GU17 13 F2
Barbon CI GU15 15 G2
Bardsley Dr GU9 34 B6
Barford CI GU51 23 H1
Barge CI GU11 26 B4
Barkis Mead GU47 6 D1
Barley Way GU51 17 F2
Barn CI GU15 8 B5
Barn Fld GU46 3 D3
Barn Meadow CI GU52 22 D6
Barnard CI GU16 14 C5
Barnard Way GU11 25 F6
Barncroft GU9 34 D4
Barnes CI GU14 20 A3
Barnes Rd GU16 14 B5
Barnett La GU18 10 A4
Barnsford Cres GU24 11 G5
Barnsley CI GU15 21 E6
Barossa Rd GU15 8 A4
Barrack Rd GU11 31 F1
Barrie Rd GU9 30 A4
Barton CI GU11 31 E2
Bartons Dr GU46 3 D4
Bartons Way GU14 12 C6
Basing Dr GU11 31 H5
Basingbourne CI GU52 23 E3
Basingbourne Rd GU52 23 E4
Basset CI GU16 14 C5
Bat and Ball La GU10 36 D2
Bateman Gro GU12 32 C3
Bath Rd GU15 8 A5
Bayfield Av GU16 14 C6
Bayford CI GU17 13 F4
Baywood CI GU14 18 B2
Beacon CI GU10 36 D3
Beacon Hill Rd GU52 23 G4
Beales La GU10 36 C1
Beam Hollow GU9 30 C4
Bear La GU11 31 G1
Bearwood Cotts GU10 36 C1
Bearwood Gdns GU51 17 E6
Beaufort Rd, Aldershot GU12 26 C4
Beaufort Rd, Church Crookham GU52 23 F3
Beaufort Rd, Farnham GU9 34 D2
Beaufront CI GU15 9 E4
Beaufront Rd GU15 9 E4
Beaulieu Ct GU17 6 B6
Beaulieu Gdns GU17 6 B5
Beaumaris Par GU16 14 D5
Beaumont Gro GU11 31 E1
Beaver La GU46 3 E3
Beavers CI GU9 34 B3
Beavers Hill GU9 34 A3
Beavers Rd GU9 34 B3
Bechin CI GU52 22 C6
Beck Gdns GU16 30 B5
Bedford Av GU16 20 C2
Bedford Cres GU16 20 C1
Bedford La GU16 20 C2
Beech Av, Camberley GU15 14 B1
Beech Av, Farnham GU9 37 F2
Beech Dr GU17 12 D1
Beech Rd, Camberley GU16 20 C1
Beech Rd, Farnborough GU14 13 G6
Beech Ride, Fleet GU52 22 D2
Beech Ride, Sandhurst GU47 6 B2
Beech Tree Dr GU9 31 G6

Beechbrook Av GU46 3
Beeching CI GU12 33
Beechnut Dr GU17 6
Beechnut Ind Est GU11 31
Beechnut Rd GU13 31
Beechwood CI GU51 22
Beetons Av GU12 26
Beldam Bridge Rd GU24 11
Beldham Rd GU9 34
Belgrave Ct GU17 12
Bell CI GU14 20
Bell La, Camberley GU17 6
Bell La, Rowledge GU10 36
Bell Pl GU19 4
Belland Dr GU11 31
Belle Vue CI GU12 32
Belle Vue Enterprise Centre GU12 32
Belle Vue Rd GU12 32
Bellever Hill GU15 8
Bellew Rd GU16 15
Bellingham CI GU15 15
Belmont CI GU14 13
Belmont Mws GU14 13
Belmont Rd GU15 13
Belsize Rd GU14 19
Belstone Mws GU14 13
Belton Rd GU15 8
Belvedere CI GU13 16
Belvedere Ct GU17 12
Belvedere Rd GU14 20
Belvoir CI GU16 14
Benner La GU24 11
Bennett Ct GU15 7
Bentley Copse GU15 15
Bentley Dr GU51 16
Beresford CI GU16 20
Bergenia Ct GU24 11
Berkeley CI GU51 17
Berkeley Cres GU14 14
Berkshire Rd GU15 8
Bernersh CI GU47 6
Berrybank GU47 6
Beta CI GU14 19
Bethel CI GU9 30
Bethel La GU9 30
Betjeman Walk GU46 3
Beveren CI GU51 17
Beverley CI, Aldershot GU12 32
Beverley CI, Camberley GU15 9
Beverley Cres GU14 19
Bicknell Rd GU16 14
Bideford CI GU14 13
Bietigheim Way GU15 8
Binfields GU9 34
Binsted Dr GU17 6
Birch Av GU51 17
Birch CI, Camberley GU15 8
Birch CI, Farnham GU10 36
Birch Dr GU17 12
Birch La GU24 11
Birch Par GU51 17
Birch Platt GU24 11
Birch Rd GU20 5
Birch Tree Vw GU18 10
Birch Way GU12 26
Birchett Rd, Aldershot GU11 31
Birchett Rd, Farnborough GU14 19
Birchfields GU15 13
Birchlands Ct GU47 7
Birchview GU46 3
Birchwood Dr GU18 10
Birdhaven GU10 36
Birdwood Rd GU15 7
Birkbeck Pl GU47 7
Bishop Sumner Dr GU9 34
Bishops CI GU52 23
Bishops Gro GU20 5
Bishops Mead GU9 34
Bishops Rd GU9 30
Bittern CI GU47 7

ck Pond La GU10 37 F1
ckbird GU10 6 D3
ckbushe Bsns Centre
J46 3 C4
ckbushes Rd GU51 16 D1
ckcap Pl GU47 6 D3
ckdown Rd GU16 15 F6
ckheath Rd GU9 30 A4
ckstone Cl GU14 18 D1
ckstroud La East
J18 11 E3
ckthorn Cres GU14 13 E5
ckthorn Dr GU18 10 B4
ckwater Cl GU12 32 D2
ck Pk GU12 6 B2
ckwater Valley Rd
J12 14 A6
ckwater Way GU12 32 B3
ckwater Way Ind Est
J12 32 B3
ne Pk GU46 3 B1
se Cl GU14 20 B4
xes Ride GU46 3 B2
nheim Cl GU10 32 C4
nheim Cres GU9 30 A6
nheim Ct GU14 20 B5
nheim Pk GU11 25 H2
nheim Rd GU11 25 H2
d La GU24 11 F2
omsbury Way
J17 12 C2
e Pryor Ct GU52 22 D6
ebell Rise GU18 10 B3
ebell Walk*,
ockton Pk GU51 17 E5
throat Ct GU47 6 D3
ff Cove GU11 26 A6
nden Rd GU14 19 E3
hwood Dr GU16 14 B3
ding House La
J24 11 G5
derside GU46 3 A2
elli Mws GU9 34 C3
elli Yd*,
rrelli Mws GU9 34 D3
rowdale Gdns
J15 9 G6
man Dr GU20 5 F1
lters Rd GU12 31 H2
ndary Rd,
rnborough GU14 20 A5
ndary Rd,
wledge GU10 36 B6
ndstone Cl GU10 37 E2
ndstone Rd GU14 36 B4
rley La GU10 30 A1
rley Rd GU52 23 G5
rne Dene GU10 36 D2
rne Firs GU10 37 G2
rne Gro GU10 35 E6
rne Grove Cl GU10 35 F6
rne Grove Dr
J10 37 G1
rne Mill Ind Est
J9 31 G3
enhurst Gdns
J52 23 E5
enhurst La GU10 28 A2
enhurst Rd GU52 23 E4
ver Rd GU10 36 D2
wling Alley GU10 28 A2
wling Green Ct
J16 14 C6
alls Gro GU11 31 G4
alls La GU11 31 F4
oon Rd GU14 19 F2
cebridge GU15 7 G6
cken La GU46 3 A2
ckendale Cl GU16 14 B2
ckendale Rd GU15 14 A6
ckendene GU12 27 F6
ckenwood GU15 9 G6
cklesham Cl GU14 19 G1
cknell Cl GU15 8 D2
cknell Rd,
cshot GU19 4 B2
cknell Rd,
mberley GU15 8 D2
emar Cl GU16 14 D5
nble Bank GU16 20 D2
mbles Cl GU12 33 E2
mbleton Av GU9 34 C6
mblewood Pl
J51 22 C1
ncote GU15 9 F6
nley La GU11 6 B6
nley Rd GU15 13 G3
nling Av GU46 3 B2

Bramshot Dr GU51 17 F5
Bramshot La,
Farnborough GU14 18 C1
Bramshot La,
Fleet GU51 18 A3
Bramshot Rd GU14 18 A6
Brandon Cl GU15 15 G1
Brandon Rd GU52 22 C5
Branksome Cl GU15 8 B5
Branksome Ct GU51 16 D6
Branksome Hill Rd
GU47 7 E4
Branksome Park Rd
GU15 8 B5
Bransemewood Rd
GU51 16 D6
Braye Cl GU47 6 C2
Breach La GU47 6 A3
Brecon Cl GU14 12 D6
Brendon Rd GU14 12 D6
Brentmoor Rd GU24 11 E5
Brewers Cl GU14 19 F3
Briar Av GU18 10 A4
Briarleas Ct GU14 26 B1
Briars Cl GU14 18 D4
Bricksbury Hill GU9 30 C4
Bridge End GU15 13 H1
Bridge Rd,
Aldershot GU11 31 G3
Bridge Rd,
Bagshot GU19 4 C5
Bridge Rd,
Camberley GU15 13 G2
Bridge Rd,
Farnborough GU14 19 F3
Bridge Walk GU46 3 D1
Bridge Works GU15 13 G2
Bridgefield GU9 35 E3
Bridgemead GU16 14 A5
Bridle Ct GU11 31 E2
Bright Ct GU46 3 D3
Brighton Rd GU12 32 A4
Brightwells Rd GU9 34 D3
Brindle Cl GU11 31 G4
Brinksway GU51 23 E1
Brinns La GU17 6 C6
Bristow Rd GU15 13 H2
Brittain Ct GU47 6 C4
Britten Cl GU12 33 E1
Broad Ha'Penny GU10 36 D3
Broad St GU14 11 E4
Broad Walk GU16 14 C3
Broadacres GU51 22 C2
Broadhurst GU14 18 B3
Broadlands,
Camberley GU16 14 D5
Broadlands,
Farnborough GU14 20 B5
Bradley Grn GU20 5 H5
Broadmead GU15 18 D5
Broadway Rd GU20 5 G6
Broadwell Rd GU10 36 C2
Brockenhurst Dr GU14 3 D4
Brockenhurst Rd
GU11 31 G3
Brockhurst Lodge GU9 37 F1
Brocklands GU46 3 B4
Brokle Cl GU52 22 C6
Brook Av GU9 31 F4
Brook Cl,
Aldershot GU12 33 E1
Brook Cl,
Owlsmoor GU47 7 E2
Brook Gdns GU15 19 E5
Brook Rd,
Bagshot GU19 4 C5
Brook Rd,
Camberley GU15 13 G1
Brooke Ct GU16 20 D1
Brookfield Rd GU12 32 C1
Brookhouse Rd GU14 19 E4
Brooklands GU11 31 E2
Brooklands Cl GU9 30 D4
Brooklands Rd GU9 30 D5
Brooklands Way GU9 30 D5
Brookly Gdns GU51 17 F6
Brookmead Ct GU9 34 C4
Brooksby Cl GU17 6 B6
Brookside,
Farnham GU9 30 C5
Brookside,
Sandhurst GU47 6 C4
Brookside Pk GU14 13 G4
Brookwood Rd GU14 20 B3
Broom Acres,
Fleet GU52 23 E3
Broom Acres,
Sandhurst GU47 6 B3

Broom Cl GU17 12 D1
Broom Fld GU18 10 B4
Broome Cl GU46 3 C1
Broomhill GU10 29 F4
Broomhill Rd GU14 18 D2
Broomleaf Cnr GU9 35 E4
Broomleaf Rd GU9 35 E4
Broomrigg Rd GU51 16 C5
Broomsquires Rd GU19 4 C6
Broomwood Way
GU10 37 F1
Brougham Pl GU9 30 B4
Broughton Mws GU16 14 C4
Browning Cl GU14 15 F1
Browning Rd GU52 22 C6
Browns Walk GU10 36 C4
Brownsover Rd GU14 18 C3
Brunswick Rd GU16 21 F1
Bruntile Cl GU14 20 B6
Bryanstone Cl GU52 23 F4
Bryce Gdns GU11 32 A5
Bryn Rd GU10 36 C1
Buckhurst Rd GU16 21 E2
Buckingham Way
GU16 14 C5
Buckland Cl GU14 13 H6
Buller Ct GU14 25 H1
Buller Rd GU11 25 G5
Bullers Rd GU9 31 E6
Bullfinch Cl GU47 6 D3
Burdock Cl GU18 10 C3
Burford Rd GU15 13 G1
Burghead Cl GU47 6 D3
Burgoyne Rd GU15 8 D5
Burleigh Rd GU16 14 A5
Burley Way GU17 6 C5
Burlington Ct,
Aldershot GU11 31 F2
Burlington Ct,
Blackwater GU17 12 C2
Burne-Jones Dr GU47 6 D5
Burnet Ct GU24 11 E5
Burns Av GU52 23 G3
Burns Cl GU14 19 F1
Burnsall Cl GU14 19 G1
Burnside GU51 17 E6
Burnt Hill Rd GU10 36 D1
Burnt Hill Way GU10 37 E3
Burnt Pollard La GU24 11 H2
Burrell Rd GU16 14 A5
Burrwood Gdns GU12 26 D5
Burton Cl GU20 5 G4
Busk Cres GU14 19 F4
Butler Rd GU19 4 D6
Buttermer Cl GU10 36 C1
Buttermere Cl GU14 13 H6
Buttermere Ct*,
Lakeside GU12 26 C5
Buttermere Dr GU15 9 G6
Byron Cl GU15 19 E2
Byron Cl, Fleet GU51 23 E1
Byron Cl, Yateley GU46 3 B4
Byways GU46 3 B3
Byworth Cl GU9 34 A3
Byworth Rd GU9 34 A4

Cabrol Rd GU14 19 G2
Cadet Way GU52 23 F5
Cadnam Cl GU11 31 H5
Cadogan Rd GU11 26 B2
Caernavon Cl GU16 14 D5
Caesar Ct GU11 31 E2
Caesars Camp Rd
GU16 8 D3
Caesars Cl GU15 8 D3
Caesars Ct,
Camberley GU15 8 D3
Caesars Ct,
Farnham GU9 30 C5
Cairn Cl GU16 15 F2
Cairngorm Cl GU14 13 E6
Calcott Pk GU46 3 A2
Caldwell Rd GU20 5 H3
Calshot Way GU16 14 D6
Calthorpe Cl GU51 16 C5
Calthorpe Sq GU51 23 E1
Calton Gdns GU11 32 A4
Calvert Cl GU12 32 B3
Calvin Cl GU15 19 E2
Cambrian Cl GU15 7 H6
Cambrian Rd GU14 18 D1
Cambridge Pl GU9 34 D3
Cambridge Rd,
Aldershot GU11 31 F1
Cambridge Rd,
Owlsmoor GU47 7 E2
Cambridge Rd West
GU14 19 H6
Cambridge Walk GU15 8 A5

Camden Walk GU51 17 G6
Camellia Ct GU24 11 F5
Cameron Rd GU11 26 A2
Camp Farm Rd GU11 26 A4
Camp Rd GU14 26 A1
Campbell Cl,
Aldershot GU11 31 H5
Campbell Cl,
Fleet GU51 22 D1
Campbell Cl,
Yateley GU46 3 F3
Campbell Pl GU16 14 C2
Campbell Rd GU11 25 F6
Campion Cl GU17 13 F2
Camus Cl GU52 22 C5
Canada Rd GU16 15 G5
Canal Cl GU11 26 B4
Canal Cotts GU12 26 D5
Canberra Cl GU16 3 A1
Canning Rd GU12 32 A1
Cannon Cl GU47 7 E3
Canterbury Rd,
Ash GU12 26 D6
Canterbury Rd,
Farnborough GU14 20 A5
Capper Rd GU15 7 G4
Carfax Av GU10 32 C3
Cargate Av GU11 31 F2
Cargate Gro GU11 31 F3
Cargate Hill GU11 31 F2
Cargate Ter GU11 31 F2
Carisbrooke GU16 14 C5
Carlinwark Dr GU15 8 C4
Carlton Cl GU16 15 E2
Carlton Cres GU52 23 F3
Carlyon Cl,
Farnborough GU14 20 A4
Carlyon Cl,
Mychett GU16 20 C3
Carmarthen Cl GU14 13 F6
Carnival Sq GU51 17 E6
Caroline Way GU16 14 C4
Carrick La GU46 3 E3
Carrington La GU12 26 D1
Carshalton Rd GU15 8 D2
Carters Walk GU9 30 D3
Carthona Dr GU52 23 E2
Cassino Ct GU11 31 G1
Castle Cl GU15 14 C1
Castle Ct GU9 34 C3
Castle Hill GU9 34 C2
Castle Rd,
Aldershot GU11 25 E6
Castle Rd,
Camberley GU15 14 C1
Castle St,
Farnham GU9 34 C3
Castle St, Fleet GU52 23 E2
Castlecraig Ct GU47 6 D3
Castor Ct,
Church Crookham
GU52 23 G4
Castor Ct,
Yateley GU46 3 B1
Caswall Ride GU46 3 F3
Caswell Cl GU14 19 F1
Catena Rise GU18 10 B2
Catesby Gdns GU46 3 A3
Catherine Ct*,
Queens Rd GU11 31 E1
Cavalry Ct GU11 31 E2
Cavans Rd GU11 26 A3
Cavendish Ct GU17 12 C2
Cavendish Gdns
GU52 22 D5
Cavendish Mws GU11 31 F2
Cavendish Pk GU47 7 E5
Cavendish Rd,
Aldershot GU11 31 G2
Cavendish Rd,
Fleet GU52 22 D5
Caves Farm Cl GU47 6 A3
Cedar Av GU17 6 D6
Cedar Cl,
Aldershot GU12 32 B4
Cedar Cl,
Bagshot GU19 4 B5
Cedar Dr GU51 17 H6
Cedar La GU16 14 A5
Cedar Rd GU14 19 H4
Cedarways GU9 37 E1
Celandine Ct GU46 3 A2
Celery La GU11 37 E2
Cemetery Rd GU51 22 C3
Centurion Cl GU47 6 D3
Chaffinch Cl GU47 6 D3
Chalfont Dr GU14 20 A5
Chamber La GU10 36 A1
Chambers Rd GU12 27 E4

Chamomile Gdns
GU14 18 C2
Champion Way GU52 23 E4
Chandlers La GU46 3 C1
Chandlers Rd GU12 27 E5
Chantreys GU51 22 C1
Chantry Ct GU16 14 A4
Chantry Rd GU19 4 B6
Chapel La,
Bagshot GU19 4 B6
Chapel La,
Farnborough GU14 13 E5
Chapel Rd,
Camberley GU15 7 G6
Chapel Rd,
Rowledge GU10 36 C4
Chapel Sq GU15 7 F4
Charlcote Cl GU14 20 B4
Charlotte Cl GU9 30 D4
Charlton Ct GU47 6 D2
Chart House Rd GU14 26 D2
Chartwell,
Camberley GU16 20 C2
Chartwell,
Wrecclesham GU9 36 C1
Chasewater Ct GU11 31 F2
Chatfield Cl GU14 20 A6
Chatsworth Gro GU9 30 B6
Chatsworth Heights
GU15 9 E4
Chatsworth Rd GU14 20 B4
Chaucer Gro GU15 8 A6
Chaucer Rd GU14 19 F1
Chaundlers Cft GU10 28 B6
Chawton Cl GU51 16 B4
Cherberry Cl GU51 17 F3
Cheriton Way GU17 6 D6
Cherry Tree Cl,
Farnborough GU14 18 C2
Cherry Tree Cl,
Farnham GU9 34 D3
Cherry Tree Cl,
Sandhurst GU47 6 C2
Cherry Tree Rd GU10 36 B5
Cherry Tree Walk GU10 36 B5
Cherrydale Rd GU15 9 G6
Cherryhill Gro GU11 31 E3
Cherrywood Rd GU14 13 G6
Chertsey Rd GU20 5 H4
Chesilton Cres GU52 23 E4
Chester Cl GU11 33 E1
Chester Rd GU12 33 E1
Chester Way GU10 32 C5
Chesters Rd GU15 9 E6
Chestnut Av,
Aldershot GU12 32 B4
Chestnut Av,
Camberley GU15 9 E5
Chestnut Av,
Farnham GU9 34 B6
Chestnut Cl,
Blackwater GU17 12 D1
Chestnut Cl,
Fleet GU51 17 G3
Chestnut Ct GU12 32 A1
Chestnut Gro GU51 17 F5
Chestnut Rd GU14 19 G2
Cheswell Gdns GU51 22 C3
Chetwode Pl GU12 32 A4
Chetwode Ter GU11 30 D2
Cheviot Cl,
Camberley GU15 15 F1
Cheviot Cl,
Farnborough GU14 13 E6
Cheviot Dr GU51 17 F3
Chewter Cl GU19 4 C5
Chewter La GU20 5 F1
Cheylesmore Dr GU16 15 G2
Cheyne Way GU14 13 F6
Chicheley Cl GU14 19 G1
Chichester Rd GU12 26 D6
Chilham Cl GU16 14 C5
Chillingham Way
GU15 13 H1
Chiltern Av GU14 18 D3
Chiltern Cl,
Church Crookham
GU52 23 F4
Chiltern Cl,
Farnborough GU14 18 C3
Chineham Cl GU51 16 B4
Chingford Av GU14 20 A2
Chinnock Cl GU52 22 D2
Chippendale Cl GU17 12 D1
Chive Cl GU14 18 B3
Chobham Rd GU16 14 B4
Chrismas Av GU12 32 A3
Chrismas Pl GU12 32 A3

Christchurch Cl GU52 22 D5
Christchurch Dr GU17 6 C5
Christie Cl GU18 10 C2
Christie Walk GU46 3 C4
Christine Cl GU12 32 C3
Christy Est GU12 32 B2
Church Av GU14 20 A6
Church Circle GU14 20 A6
Church Ct GU51 16 D6
Church Gro GU51 16 D6
Church Hill,
 Aldershot GU12 31 H3
Church Hill,
 Camberley GU15 8 B6
Church Hill Ter GU18 28 B5
Church La,
 Aldershot GU11 31 H3
Church La, Ash GU12 33 E2
Church La,
 Ewshot GU10 29 F2
Church La,
 Farnborough GU14 18 D3
Church La,
 Rowledge GU10 36 B5
Church La,
 Wrecclesham GU10 36 C1
Church La East GU11 31 G3
Church La West GU11 31 F3
Church Mws GU46 3 D1
Church Pass*,
 The Borough GU9 34 C4
Church Path,
 Aldershot GU12 27 E6
Church Path,
 Ash GU12 33 E1
Church Path,
 Farnborough GU14 20 A3
Church Path,
 North Camp GU14 26 A1
Church Path,
 West Heath GU14 19 E3
Church Rd,
 Aldershot GU11 31 H4
Church Rd,
 Bagshot GU19 4 B5
Church Rd, Fleet GU51 16 D5
Church Rd,
 Frimley GU16 14 A5
Church Rd,
 Owlsmoor GU47 6 D1
Church Rd,
 West End GU24 11 F4
Church Rd,
 Windlesham GU20 5 F4
Church Rd East GU14 20 A6
Church Rd West GU14 19 H6
Church St,
 Aldershot GU11 31 H4
Church St,
 Crondall GU10 28 B5
Church Vw, Ash GU12 32 D1
Church Vw,
 Yateley GU46 3 D1
Churchdale*,
 St Josephs Rd GU11 31 G3
Churchill Av GU12 31 H3
Churchill Cl GU14 13 G5
Churchill Cres,
 Farnborough GU14 13 G6
Churchill Cres,
 Yateley GU46 3 D3
Clandon Ct GU14 20 B5
Clanfield Ride GU17 6 D6
Clare Ct*,
 Clarence Rd GU51 23 E1
Clare Mead GU10 36 C4
Claremont Av GU15 8 C6
Clarence Cl GU12 32 A1
Clarence Ct*,
 Clarence Rd GU51 17 E6
Clarence Dr GU15 9 E4
Clarence Rd GU51 17 E6
Clarendon Ct GU17 12 C2
Clarendon Ho*,
 Birch Av GU51 17 E6
Clarewood Dr GU15 8 B5
Clarke Cres GU15 7 E4
Claycart Rd GU11 24 D6
Claydon Gdns GU17 13 F4
Clayton Rd GU14 13 E5
Clearsprings GU18 10 A2
Clevedon Cl GU14 20 B4
Clevedon Ct GU14 14 D5
Clewborough Dr GU15 9 E5
Clifton Cl GU10 36 D6
Clifton Gdns GU16 20 C1
Clive Rd GU12 32 A1
Clockhouse Rd GU14 19 G3
Closeworth Rd GU14 26 B1

Clouston Rd GU14 19 F2
Clover La GU46 3 A2
Clubhouse Rd GU11 25 E5
Clumps Rd GU10 37 G3
Coach House Cl GU16 14 B2
Coach House Gdns
 GU51 17 E4
Coachmans Gro GU47 6 B4
Cobbetts La GU46 3 F3
Cobbetts Way GU9 36 C1
Cochrane Pl GU47 5 G3
Cock-a-Dobby GU47 6 A2
Cody Cl GU12 26 C4
Cody Rd GU14 19 F4
Cody Technology Pk
 GU14 18 A6
Coe Cl GU14 31 F2
Cokenor Wood GU10 36 C2
Colbeck GU52 23 F5
Cold Harbour La GU14 13 E5
Coldharbour La GU24 11 F3
Cole Av GU11 31 F1
Colebred Cnr GU51 17 G3
Coleford Bridge Rd
 GU16 20 B3
Coleford Cl GU16 20 C4
Coleman Rd GU12 32 A3
Coleridge Av GU46 3 E3
Coleson Hill Rd GU10 36 C2
Coleville Rd GU14 19 F2
Coliseum Bsns Centre
 GU15 13 F2
College Cl GU15 8 B3
College Cres GU47 7 E3
College Gdns GU9 34 C3
College Pl GU9 34 D4
College Rd, Ash GU12 27 E6
College Rd,
 College Town GU47 7 E4
College Ride,
 Bagshot GU19 4 A6
College Ride,
 Camberley GU15 8 A4
Collier Cl GU14 18 D2
Collingwood Gd GU14 20 B6
Collingwood Grange Cl
 GU15 9 E3
Collingwood Rise
 GU15 9 E4
Collins Gdns GU12 33 E2
Colne Way GU12 32 D2
Columbus Dr GU14 18 C3
Colville Gdns GU18 10 C3
Colwyn Cl GU46 3 B2
Combe La GU14 19 F1
Combe Rise GU10 37 G3
Comet Cl GU12 26 C4
Comfrey Cl GU14 18 D2
Commercial Rd GU12 32 A3
Commodore Ct GU14 25 H1
Commonfields GU24 11 F5
Compound Rd GU14 19 G5
Compton Cl,
 Church Crookham
 GU52 23 F4
Compton Cl,
 Sandhurst GU47 6 C2
Compton Rd GU52 23 F4
Compton Way GU10 35 G4
Conifer Cl GU52 23 E4
Conifer Dr GU15 8 D5
Coniston Cl,
 Camberley GU15 15 F2
Coniston Cl,
 Farnborough GU14 19 E4
Coniston Cl,
 Lightwater GU18 10 C2
Coniston Ct*, Lakeside Cl,
 Ash GU12 26 C5
Coniston Dr GU9 30 A5
Coniston Way GU14 22 D5
Connaught Cl GU46 3 B2
Connaught Rd,
 Aldershot GU12 32 A2
Connaught Rd,
 Bagshot GU19 4 A5
Connaught Rd,
 Camberley GU15 8 C6
Connaught Rd,
 Fleet GU51 17 E6
Connop Way GU16 14 D2
Consort Dr GU15 9 F4
Constable Way GU47 7 E5
Constant Rd GU14 19 G5
Constantius Ct GU52 22 C6
Conway Cl GU16 14 C4
Conway Dr GU14 19 E4
Cookham Cl GU47 6 C2
Coolarne Rise GU15 8 D5

Coombe Cl GU16 14 B5
Coombe Dr GU51 17 G6
Coombe Rd GU46 3 B1
Cooper Rd GU20 5 G4
Coopers Ter GU9 34 D2
Copelands Cl GU15 15 G1
Copped Hall Dr GU15 9 F5
Copped Hall Way GU15 9 F5
Copperfield Av GU47 6 D1
Coppice Cl GU15 31 E5
Coppice Gdns GU46 3 C3
Copse Av GU14 31 E4
Copse Cl GU15 8 D5
Copse End,
 Camberley GU15 8 D5
Copse End,
 Fleet GU51 22 B1
Copse La, Fleet GU52 22 C4
Copse La,
 Yateley GU46 3 B1
Copse Way GU10 36 C2
Copthorne Dr GU18 10 C2
Corbett Dr GU18 10 A4
Cordelia Gdns GU12 26 C1
Cordwalles Rd GU15 8 C3
Corfe Gdns GU16 14 C4
Corfe Way GU14 20 B6
Coriander Cl GU14 18 C3
Cormorant Pl GU47 6 D4
Cornbunting Cl GU47 6 D4
Cornelia Cl GU14 18 D4
Cornfields GU46 3 B4
Cornwall Cl GU15 8 C4
Coronation Rd,
 Aldershot GU11 31 H4
Coronation Rd,
 Yateley GU46 3 E1
Corringway GU52 23 F3
Cotswold Cl GU14 13 E6
Cotswold Cl GU51 23 E1
Cottage Gdns GU14 19 F3
Cotton Cl GU11 31 F1
Cottrell Cl GU52 22 D5
Cottrell Flats GU14 26 B1
Court Dr GU52 23 F3
Court Gdns GU15 8 A6
Court Rd GU11 31 G1
Courtenay Rd GU9 31 E5
Courtmoor Av GU52 23 E2
Cove Rd,
 Farnborough GU14 19 E3
Cove Rd, Fleet GU51 17 F4
Coverts Cl GU9 35 F2
Covey Cl GU14 19 E4
Cox Grn GU47 6 D5
Coxbridge Mdws GU9 34 A4
Coxheath Rd GU52 22 C3
Coxmoor Cl GU52 23 G4
Crabtree Rd GU15 13 G3
Crake Pl GU47 6 D5
Cranberry Walk GU14 13 F2
Cranbrook Ct GU51 17 E5
Crane Ct GU47 6 D3
Cranford Av GU52 22 D4
Cranford Park Dr GU46 3 D2
Cranleigh Ct GU14 19 E4
Cranmore Cl GU11 30 D2
Cranmore Ct GU16 20 D3
Cranmore Gdns GU11 30 D3
Cranmore La GU11 30 D2
Cranmore Rd GU16 20 D3
Cranwell Gro GU18 10 A3
Craven Cl GU14 37 F1
Crawford Gdns GU15 7 G6
Crawley Dr GU15 8 C5
Crawley Hill GU15 8 C6
Crawley Ridge GU15 8 C5
Crawley Wood Cl GU15 8 C6
Credon Cl GU14 19 E2
Crees Mdw GU20 5 G4
Crerar Cl GU14 18 C4
Crescent La GU12 27 E5
Cricket La GU10 37 G2
Cricketers La GU20 5 H3
Crimea Rd GU11 31 G1
Cripley Rd GU12 18 D2
Croft La,
 Crondall GU10 28 A6
Croft La, Yateley GU46 3 C1
Croft Rd GU11 31 H3
Croft Way GU16 14 C4
Crofters Cl GU47 6 A3
Cromwell Rd GU15 8 A4
Cromwell Way GU14 13 H6
Crondall Ct GU15 13 H1
Crondall End GU46 3 C1
Crondall La GU9 34 A3
Crondall Rd GU51 22 A4
Crookham Rd GU51 22 D2

Crookham Reach
 GU52 22 C4
Cropleigh Ct GU14 19 H3
Crosby Gdns GU46 3 A1
Crosby Hill Dr GU15 8 C4
Crosby Way GU9 34 B4
Cross Gdns GU16 20 C1
Cross La GU16 20 C1
Cross Rd GU12 27 E6
Cross St,
 Aldershot GU11 31 G1
Cross St,
 Farnborough GU14 25 H1
Crossways,
 Aldershot GU12 32 A3
Crossways,
 Crookham Village
 GU51 22 B4
Crown Dr GU9 31 F6
Crown Gdns GU51 23 F1
Crown La,
 Aldershot GU11 31 H1
Crown La,
 Farnham GU9 31 F6
Crown Pl GU47 6 D2
Crowthorne Rd GU47 6 A3
Croyde Cl GU14 19 F1
Cruikshank Lea GU47 7 E5
Crundwell Ct GU9 34 D2
Cuckoo La GU24 11 E5
Cuckoo Vale GU24 10 D5
Cullen Cl GU46 3 C3
Cullens Mws GU11 31 F2
Culver Rd GU47 6 D2
Culverlands Cres
 GU12 26 D6
Cumberland Rd GU15 15 F1
Cumbria Ct GU14 20 B6
Cunnington Rd GU14 20 B6
Curley Hill Rd GU18 9 H4
Curly Bridge Cl GU14 13 F5
Curtis Cl GU15 9 F4
Curtis Ct GU15 23 E4
Curzon Dr GU52 23 F4
Cuthbert Rd GU12 27 E3
Cutts Rd GU11 26 B3
Cygnet Ct GU15 17 F4
Cypress Dr GU51 17 H6
Cypress Gro GU12 26 D2
Cypress Way GU17 6 B6
Cyprus Rd GU16 15 G5

Dale Cl GU10 36 C1
Dale Gdns GU47 6 A3
Dalley Ct GU47 6 D4
Dalston Cl GU15 15 G2
Damask Cl GU24 11 F5
Danebury Walk GU16 14 C5
Danvers Dr GU52 22 C6
Daphne Dr GU52 22 D6
Darby Green La GU17 6 B6
Darby Green Rd GU17 6 A6
Dares La GU10 28 D2
Dark La GU20 5 E4
Darleydale Cl GU47 6 D1
Darracott Cl GU15 9 F3
Darset Av GU51 17 F5
Dart Rd GU14 18 D1
Darvills La GU9 34 D3
Darwin Gro GU11 26 A6
David Sq GU52 23 E3
Davis Gdns GU47 7 E4
Dawnay Rd GU15 7 G3
Dawsmere Cl GU15 9 F6
Deadbrook La GU12 26 B6
Dean Cl GU12 33 F1
Dean Par GU15 8 C3
Deans Ct GU20 5 G4
Decouttere Cl GU52 22 C5
Deedman Cl GU12 32 D1
Deep Well Dr GU15 8 B6
Deepcut Bridge Rd
 GU16 15 F6
Deepdene GU10 37 G1
Deer Leap GU18 10 B3
Deer Rock Rd GU15 8 C4
Dell Gro GU16 14 D1
Delville Rd GU14 18 D4
Denby Dene GU12 33 E1
Dene Cl GU12 33 F1
Dene La GU10 37 G1
Dene La West GU10 37 G1
Dene Rd GU14 19 F4
Dene Walk GU10 37 G1
Denham Dr GU16 14 D3
Denly Way GU18 10 C2
Denman Cl GU12 23 G1
Denmark Sq GU12 32 B1
Denmark St GU12 32 B1

Denning Cl GU52 22[cut]
Dennistoun Cl GU15 8[cut]
Denton Way GU16 14[cut]
Derek Horn Ct GU15 7[cut]
Derry Cl GU12 13[cut]
Derwent Av GU12 26[cut]
Derwent Cl,
 Farnborough GU14 18[cut]
Derwent Cl,
 Farnham GU9 30[cut]
Derwent Rd GU18 10[cut]
Dettingen Rd GU16 15[cut]
Devon Cl, Fleet GU51 17[cut]
Devon Cl,
 Sandhurst GU47 6[cut]
Devonshire Dr GU15 8[cut]
Devonshire Pl GU11 31[cut]
Dexter Way GU51 17[cut]
Diamond Hill GU15 8[cut]
Diamond Ridge GU15 8[cut]
Dickens Way GU46 3[cut]
Dinorben Av GU14 22[cut]
Dinorben Beeches
 GU52 22[cut]
Dinorben Cl GU52 22[cut]
Dippenhall St GU10 28[cut]
Dogflud Way GU9 34[cut]
Dollis Dr GU9 35[cut]
Doman Rd GU15 13[cut]
Donnington Cl GU15 13[cut]
Doras Green La GU10 29[cut]
Dorcas Ct GU15 13[cut]
Doreen Cl GU14 12[cut]
Dorset Ct GU15 8[cut]
Dorset Rd GU12 27[cut]
Douai Cl GU14 20[cut]
Douglas Gro GU10 37[cut]
Douglas Pl GU14 19[cut]
Dovedale Cl GU47 6[cut]
Downing St GU9 34[cut]
Downs Cl GU14 12[cut]
Doyle Gdns GU46 3[cut]
Dragoon Ct GU11 31[cut]
Drake Av GU16 20[cut]
Drayhorse Dr GU19 4[cut]
Drovers End GU51 17[cut]
Drovers Way,
 Ash GU14 33[cut]
Drovers Way,
 Farnham GU9 30[cut]
Dryden Rd GU14 19[cut]
Du Maurier Cl GU52 22[cut]
Dudley Ct GU52 23[cut]
Duke of Connaughts Rd,
 Aldershot GU11 26[cut]
Duke of Connaughts Rd,
 Aldershot GU11 26[cut]
Duke of Cornwall Av
 GU15 8[cut]
Dukes Cl GU15 30[cut]
Dukes Covert GU19 4[cut]
Dukes Mead GU13 16[cut]
Dukes Pk GU11 26[cut]
Dukes Walk GU9 30[cut]
Dumas Cl GU46 3[cut]
Dunbar Rd GU16 14[cut]
Dundaff Cl GU15 8[cut]
Dungells Farm Cl
 GU46 3[cut]
Dungells La GU46 3[cut]
Dunley Dr GU51 16[cut]
Dunmow Hill GU51 17[cut]
Dunsmore Gdns GU46 3[cut]
Dunstall Pk GU14 13[cut]
Durham Rd GU47 7[cut]
Durnsford Av GU52 23[cut]
Duval Pl GU19 4[cut]

Eagles Nest GU47 6[cut]
Earls Gro GU15 8[cut]
Earlsbourne GU9 23[cut]
East Av GU9 30[cut]
East Grn GU17 12[cut]
East Ring GU10 38[cut]
East St GU9 34[cut]
East Station Rd GU12 31[cut]
Eastern Rd GU12 32[cut]
Eastmead GU14 19[cut]
Eaton Rd GU15 13[cut]
Echo Barn La GU10 36[cut]
Eddy Rd GU12 32[cut]
Edgbarrow Rise GU47 6[cut]
Edgemoor Rd GU16 15[cut]
Edinburgh Cl GU12 26[cut]
Edney Cl GU52 23[cut]
Edward Av GU15 7[cut]
Edward Ct GU14 19[cut]
Edward Rd,
 Farnham GU9 34[cut]

ard Rd,
 ndlesham GU20 5 H4
ard St GU11 31 F1
oor Plain Rd
 11 24 D5
ershot GU11 24 C5
oor Rd,
 nborough GU14 19 F5
oor Rd Trading Est
 14 19 F5
ton GU15 7 E5
ars Ct GU12 31 H2
ars Hill GU11 31 F4
eton Cl GU52 22 D5
d Rd GU12 32 A3
r Gro GU14 20 B6
n Dr GU10 37 G2
a Way GU16 14 D6
Cl GU15 9 E3
beth Av GU19 4 D6
beth GU52 23 E4
beth Par GU46 3 A2
ay GU12 26 D5
Cl GU14 19 H5
Quarters GU14 19 H5
Rd GU14 19 E5
tt Ind Pk GU12 32 B1
on Way GU10 32 C5
Bank GU46 3 C1
Cres GU9 30 C4
Ct GU47 7 E1
Gro GU9 19 G3
La GU10 32 C4
Pl GU11 31 H4
Rd GU9 30 C5
Vw GU12 27 E6
roft Cl GU16 20 C1
Rd,
 ershot GU11 31 G2
Rd, Fleet GU51 23 G1
leigh Rd GU14 19 F4
nwood Cres GU15 8 D4
nwood Dr GU15 8 D4
y Cl GU16 20 C1
n Pl GU12 31 H3
n Rd GU12 31 H4
ham Cl GU15 17 E4
ham Cres GU51 16 B4
ham Heath Way
 51 16 B5
ham Pl GU15 16 D5
ham Rd GU13 16 B5
l GU16 14 D6
ydown La GU51 16 B4
ress Av GU14 19 H2
ld Rd GU12 27 E4
esfield GU15 9 F6
rdale Gro GU9 30 A5
prise Est GU12 26 C2
m Cl GU15 7 H3
Cl GU24 11 F5
st Cl GU10 37 E1
r Rd GU15 9 E2
ale Ct*,
 eside Cl GU12 26 C5
le Way GU15 15 F1
x Cl GU16 14 D6
x Ct GU14 25 H1
n Av GU11 31 H4
n Woods Rd
 1 26 A3
ode Way GU47 6 C3
st Rd GU15 8 A2
reen Rd GU16 14 D3
ley Dr GU16 16 B4
ham Walk GU47 6 C2
Cl GU12 33 E1
0 29 F4
ot La GU52 22 D6
r Gdns GU46 3 B1
r Rd GU12 26 D6
cres GU10 36 C4
ax Ind Est GU12 32 B2
x Mws GU20 20 A6
x Rd GU14 13 H6
ld Dr GU16 14 C2
ld La GU24 11 G4
olme Gdns GU9 23 F2
Cl GU12 33 E1
ead Cl GU47 7 E4
ile GU52 23 E3
ew Gdns GU9 30 D6
ew Rd GU14 27 E6
ay Heights GU15 9 E5

Fakenham Way GU47 6 D2
Falaise Cl GU11 31 G1
Falcon Cl GU18 10 A3
Falcon Ct GU16 14 A4
Falcon Way GU46 3 B2
Falkland Ct GU14 26 B1
Falkner Rd GU9 34 D3
Falkner Rd GU9 34 B3
Falkners Cl GU51 17 G3
Fallowfield,
 Fleet GU51 17 G3
Fallowfield,
 Yateley GU46 3 B2
Falmouth Cl GU15 15 E1
Faraday Rd GU14 20 A1
Farcrosse Cl GU47 6 C3
Fareham Dr GU46 3 B2
Faringdon Cl GU47 6 C2
Farleighwallop Dr
 GU51 16 B4
Farley Cl GU46 20 A6
Farm Cl GU46 3 D3
Farm Ct GU16 14 C3
Farm Dr GU51 17 F3
Farm La GU10 28 B6
Farm Rd,
 Aldershot GU12 32 C1
Farm Rd,
 Frimley GU16 14 C3
Farm Vw GU46 3 D3
Farm Walk GU12 33 F4
Farmhouse Way GU52 22 C5
Farnborough Bsns Centre
 GU14 19 F5
Farnborough Gate
 Retail Pk GU14 13 H6
Farnborough Ind Est
 GU14 19 G4
Farnborough Rd,
 Aldershot GU11 25 E6
Farnborough Rd,
 Farnborough GU14 19 H3
Farnborough Rd,
 Farnham GU9 30 D3
Farnborough St GU14 20 A2
Farnham Bsns Centre
 GU9 34 D2
Farnham Bsns Pk
 GU9 34 B5
Farnham By-Pass 34 A5
Farnham Park Cl GU9 30 B5
Farnham Park Dr GU9 30 B5
Farnham Rd,
 Farnham GU10 28 C2
Farnham Rd,
 Fleet GU51 23 H1
Farnham Trading Est
 GU9 35 G1
Farrell Cl GU15 13 H2
Faulkner Pl GU19 4 C4
Faversham Rd GU47 6 C2
Felbridge Cl GU16 14 D4
Fellow Green Rd GU24 11 G5
Fellow Grn GU24 11 G5
Fellows Rd GU14 20 B6
Fennel Cl GU14 18 B3
Fenns La GU24 11 E5
Fenns Yd GU9 34 B5
Fennscombe Ct GU24 11 F5
Ferbies GU52 23 E3
Fermor Dr GU11 31 F1
Fern Cl GU16 15 F2
Fern Ct GU12 32 C2
Fern Dr GU52 22 D3
Fernbrae Cl GU10 37 E5
Ferndale Rd GU52 22 D5
Ferndown Gdns GU14 19 E3
Fernhill Cl,
 Camberley GU17 13 E4
Fernhill Cl,
 Farnham GU9 30 B5
Fernhill Dr GU9 30 B5
Fernhill La,
 Camberley GU17 13 E4
Fernhill La,
 Farnham GU9 30 B5
Fernhill Rd,
 Blackwater GU17 12 D3
Fernhill Rd,
 Farnborough GU14 13 E5
Fernhill Walk GU17 13 F4
Ferniehurst GU15 14 C1
Fernleigh Rise GU16 15 F6
Ferns Mead GU9 34 B4
Field End,
 Farnham GU9 35 G1
Field End,
 West End GU24 11 G5
Field La GU16 14 B4

Field Rd GU14 13 F4
Field Stores App
 GU11 25 H6
Field Way,
 Aldershot GU12 26 B6
Field Way,
 Tongham GU10 32 C4
Fieldfare Av GU46 3 B2
Fielding Rd GU47 7 E5
Fieldway GU51 22 C2
Fifield La GU10 37 F5
Findhorn Cl GU47 6 D4
Finney Dr GU20 5 G3
Fir Acre Rd GU12 26 D3
Fir Cl GU51 22 D1
Fir Dr GU17 12 D2
Fir Tree Alley GU11 31 G2
Fir Tree Way GU52 23 F1
Fircroft GU51 16 D6
Fire Station Rd GU11 25 G6
Firethorn Cl GU12 23 E3
Firfield Rd GU9 36 D1
Firglen Dr GU46 3 D2
Firgrove Ct,
 Farnborough GU14 19 H3
Firgrove Ct,
 Farnham GU9 34 D4
Firgrove Hill GU9 34 D4
Firgrove Par GU14 19 H3
Firgrove Rd,
 Farnborough GU14 19 H3
Firgrove Rd,
 Yateley GU46 3 B2
Firlands Av GU15 8 A6
Firs Cl GU14 20 A6
Firwood Dr GU15 7 H6
Fishermens Cl GU14 26 B4
Fitzroy Rd GU13 16 B5
Fiveways GU15 8 C6
Fleet Bsns Pk GU52 23 F6
Fleet Rd,
 Aldershot GU11 24 A2
Fleet Rd,
 Elvetham RG27 16 A3
Fleet Rd,
 Farnborough GU14 18 A4
Fleet Rd, Fleet GU51 17 E6
Fleming Cl GU14 20 A1
Florence Cl GU46 3 C2
Florence Rd,
 College Town GU47 6 D4
Florence Rd,
 Fleet GU51 23 F3
Foden Rd GU11 31 G2
Folly Cl GU52 23 F2
Folly Hill GU9 30 A5
Folly La North GU9 30 B5
Folly La South GU9 30 A6
Fontwell Cl GU12 32 A1
Forbes Chase GU47 6 D4
Ford La GU10 37 E1
Ford Rd GU24 11 F6
Foreman Pk GU12 33 E1
Foreman Rd GU12 33 E2
Forest Dean GU51 17 G3
Forest Dr GU10 37 F3
Forest End GU52 22 D3
Forest End Rd GU47 4 A2
Forest Glade GU10 36 B4
Forest Hills GU15 13 H1
Forge Cl GU9 35 E2
Forge Ct GU46 3 D2
Forge La GU11 25 F4
Forth Cl GU14 18 D1
Fortrose Cl GU47 6 D4
Fossewood Dr GU15 8 A3
Fosters Gro GU20 5 F2
Fowler Rd GU14 19 F5
Fowlers Rd GU11 26 A4
Fox Covert GU18 10 B3
Fox Dr GU46 3 D1
Fox Heath GU14 18 C4
Fox Hills La GU12 27 F6
Fox Rd GU10 37 F1
Fox Way GU10 29 F4
Fox Yd GU9 34 C3
Foxcroft GU52 23 F4
Foxdown Cl GU15 7 H6
Foxhill Cres GU15 9 E3
Foxhurst Rd GU12 26 D5
Foxley Cl GU17 6 C6
Foxwood GU51 17 G4
Foye La GU52 23 F4
France Hill Dr GU15 7 H6
Fraser Mead GU47 7 E5
Fraynes Cft GU51 22 D1
Frederick St GU11 31 G2
Freemantle Rd GU19 4 C4
French Gdns GU17 12 D1

Frenchmans Greek
 GU52 22 D6
Frensham Av GU51 23 G1
Frensham Cl GU46 3 B2
Frensham Ct GU10 37 E4
Frensham Heights Rd
 GU10 36 D5
Frensham Rd,
 Farnham GU9 34 D6
Frensham Rd,
 Lower Bourne GU10 37 F1
Frensham Vale GU10 37 E4
Frere Av GU51 22 C2
Freshwood Dr GU46 3 C4
Friend Av GU12 32 B2
Friesian Cl GU51 17 F3
Frimley Bsns Pk
 GU16 13 H5
Frimley Green Rd
 GU16 14 B5
Frimley Grove Gdns
 GU16 14 B4
Frimley Hall Dr GU15 8 C5
Frimley High St GU16 14 A5
Frimley Rd,
 Ash Vale GU12 26 D1
Frimley Rd,
 Camberley GU15 7 G6
Frimley Rd,
 Frimley GU16 14 A4
Frith Hill Rd GU16 14 A4
Frodsham Way GU47 7 E1
Frogmore Ct GU17 12 C1
Frogmore Gro GU17 12 C1
Frogmore Park Dr
 GU17 12 C1
Frogmore Rd GU17 6 B6
Frome Ct GU14 18 D1
Fromow Gdns GU20 5 G4
Frys Acre GU12 26 D6
Frys La, Bagshot GU19 4 B6
Frys La, Yateley GU46 3 E1
Fugelmere Rd GU51 17 G5
Fugelmere Walk GU51 17 G5
Fullers Rd GU10 36 A4
Fullerton Cl GU51 16 B4
Further Vell-Mead
 GU52 22 D6
Furze Cl GU12 26 D2
Fyfield Cl GU17 6 D6

Gables Cl GU14 19 F3
Gables Rd GU52 22 D5
Gabriel Dr GU15 15 E1
Gaffney Ct GU11 26 A2
Gainsborough Cl,
 Camberley GU15 8 C4
Gainsborough Cl,
 Farnborough GU14 20 A5
Gainsborough Ct*,
 Albert St GU51 17 E6
Gale Dr GU18 10 B2
Galley Hill Rd GU52 22 C4
Galloway Cl GU51 17 G3
Gallwey Rd GU11 25 H6
Galway Rd GU14 3 C4
Gapemouth Rd GU16 21 G2
Garbetts Way GU10 32 C5
Garden Cl GU14 18 D5
Gardeners Hill Rd
 GU10 37 E3
Gardenia Dr GU24 11 F5
Garfield Rd GU15 8 A6
Garnet Fld GU46 3 A3
Garrick Way GU16 20 C1
Garth Cl GU9 34 B6
George Gdns GU11 32 A4
George Rd GU15 23 F1
Georgeham Rd GU47 6 C1
Georgian Cl GU15 8 B4
Georgina Ct*,
 Clarence Rd GU51 17 E6
Gibbet La GU15 8 D3
Gibbons Cl GU47 6 B3
Gibbs Way GU46 3 C2
Giffard Dr GU14 19 F1
Giffards Mdw GU9 35 F4
Gilbert Rd GU16 14 A4
Gillan Av GU12 32 A3
Gillian Cl GU12 32 A3
Girton Cl GU47 7 E2
Glamis Cl GU16 14 D6
Glassonby Walk GU15 9 F6
Glebe Cl GU18 10 D2
Glebe Ct GU51 16 D6
Glebe Rd,
 Crondall GU10 28 B6
Glebe Rd,
 Farnborough GU14 19 F2

Glebeland Rd GU15 13 F1
Glen Innes GU47 7 E2
Glen Rd GU51 22 D2
Glenavon Gdns GU46 3 D4
Glencoe Cl GU16 14 D5
Glendale Pk GU13 16 B5
Gleneagles Dr GU14 18 C4
Glenhurst GU20 5 E2
Glenhurst Cl GU17 13 E1
Glenmount Rd GU16 20 D6
Glenwood GU9 30 C5
Globe Farm La GU17 6 B6
Glorney Mead GU9 31 G5
Gloster Cl GU12 26 C5
Gloucester Cl GU16 20 B1
Gloucester Gdns GU19 4 C5
Gloucester Rd,
 Aldershot GU11 31 H4
Gloucester Rd,
 Bagshot GU19 4 C5
Glynswood,
 Camberley GU15 14 C2
Glynswood,
 Wrecclesham GU10 36 D3
Goddards La GU15 13 H2
Godfrey Cl GU47 6 D4
Gold La GU11 26 B5
Goldcrest Cl GU46 3 B2
Goldfinch Cl GU11 31 F4
Goldhill GU10 37 F2
Goldney Rd GU15 15 E1
Golf Dr GU15 14 C1
Gondreville Gdns
 GU52 22 C5
Gong Hill Dr GU10 37 G4
Goodden Cres GU14 19 F5
Goodwood Cl GU15 7 H3
Goodwood Pl GU14 20 B5
Gordon Av,
 Camberley GU15 13 H1
Gordon Av,
 Fleet GU52 23 F3
Gordon Cres GU15 13 H1
Gordon Ct GU15 7 H6
Gordon Rd,
 Aldershot GU11 31 G2
Gordon Rd,
 Camberley GU15 8 A6
Gordon Rd,
 Farnborough GU14 26 A1
Gordon Walk GU46 3 F3
Gorse Bank GU18 10 B3
Gorse Cl GU10 37 E1
Gorse La GU10 37 E1
Gorse Rd GU16 14 B3
Gorselands,
 Farnham GU9 30 C4
Gorselands,
 Yateley GU46 3 C4
Gorselands Cl GU12 27 E4
Gorseway GU52 23 F2
Gort Cl GU11 26 B2
Gosden Rd GU24 11 G5
Gosnell Cl GU16 15 G2
Gothic Ct GU47 6 B3
Gough Rd GU51 16 C6
Govenors Rd GU15 7 F5
Government House Rd
 GU11 25 G2
Government Rd GU11 26 B6
Govett Gro GU20 5 H3
Gower Pk GU47 6 D4
Grace Bennett Cl
 GU14 13 F6
Grace Reynolds Walk
 GU15 8 A5
Graham Rd GU20 5 G4
Grampian Rd GU47 6 A1
Grand Av GU15 7 H5
Grange Farm Rd
 GU12 26 D6
Grange Rd, Ash GU12 33 E2
Grange Rd,
 Camberley GU15 8 C6
Grange Rd,
 Church Crookham
 GU52 22 D4
Grange Rd,
 Farnborough GU14 13 G6
Grange Rd,
 Tongham GU10 32 B6
Grantham Cl GU47 6 D2
Grantley Ct GU9 36 C1
Grantley Dr GU52 22 D2
Grasmere Rd,
 Farnborough GU14 19 E4
Grasmere Rd,
 Farnham GU9 30 A5

Grasmere Rd,
Lightwater GU18 10 B2
Gravel Rd,
Church Crookham
GU52 23 F3
Gravel Rd,
Farnborough GU14 26 B1
Gravel Rd,
Farnham GU9 30 B5
Grayshot Dr GU17 6 C6
Grayswood Dr GU16 20 D6
Great Austins GU9 35 E5
Greatfield Cl GU14 13 G6
Greatfield Rd GU14 13 G5
Green Acre GU15 31 F2
Green End GU46 3 D1
Green Farm Rd GU14 4 C5
Green Glades GU52 22 D4
Green Hill Rd GU15 9 F4
Green La,
Badshot Lea GU9 31 F6
Green La,
Bagshot GU19 4 C6
Green La,
Blackwater GU17 12 D1
Green La,
Farnham GU9 34 B6
Green La,
Frogmore GU17 12 B1
Green La,
Sandhurst GU47 6 C3
Green La,
Yateley GU46 3 B2
Green La West GU12 33 H3
Green Lane Cl GU15 7 H4
Green Leys GU52 23 E5
Green Springs GU19 28 B4
Green Way GU12 26 C6
Greenbank Way GU16 14 A4
Greencroft GU14 19 H3
Greenfield Rd GU19 34 B6
Greenhaven GU46 3 B3
Greenhill Cl,
Camberley GU15 9 F5
Greenhill Cl,
Farnham GU9 36 D1
Greenhill Rd GU16 35 E6
Greenhill Way GU9 36 D1
Greenhills GU9 35 F5
Greenholme GU15 9 G6
Greenlands Rd GU15 13 H4
Greenleas GU16 14 B3
Greenleas Cl GU46 3 C1
Greens School La
GU14 19 G3
Greensand Way GU10 35 H4
Greenways,
Fleet GU52 22 D3
Greenways,
Sandhurst GU47 6 B2
Gregan Ct GU11 31 F2
Grenadier Rd GU12 27 E5
Grenadiers Way GU14 18 C4
Grenville Dr GU51 22 C3
Grenville Gdns GU16 20 B1
Gresham Ct GU14 25 H1
Gresham Ind Est
GU12 32 B1
Gresham Way GU16 20 B1
Greville Cl GU11 31 F1
Greyhound Cl GU12 32 C2
Greys Ct GU11 31 E2
Greystead Pk GU10 36 B2
Grieve Cl GU10 32 C4
Griffon Cl GU14 18 D4
Grosvenor Ct GU17 12 D2
Grosvenor Rd GU11 31 F1
Grove Cross Rd GU14 14 B4
Grove End GU19 4 D4
Grove End Rd GU9 34 C6
Grove Rd, Ash GU12 27 E6
Grove Rd,
Camberley GU15 8 C6
Grove Rd,
Church Crookham
GU52 23 G4
Grovebell Ind Est
GU9 34 A6
Grovefields Av GU16 14 B4
Grovelands GU10 37 G1
Guernsey Dr GU51 17 F3
Guildford Rd,
Aldershot GU12 32 A4
Guildford Rd,
Ash GU12 27 G6
Guildford Rd,
Bagshot GU19 4 C5
Guildford Rd,
Farnham GU10 35 E2

Guildford Rd,
Fleet GU51 23 G1
Guildford Rd,
Frimley Green GU16 20 C1
Guildford Rd,
Lightwater GU18,19 10 B1
Guildford Rd,
West End GU24 11 E4
Guildford Rd East
GU14 20 A6
**Guildford Rd Ind
& Trading Est** GU9 35 E2
Guildford Rd West
GU14 25 H1
Guillemont Flds GU14 18 C2
Gun Hill GU11 25 G6
Gurkha Sq GU51 22 D1
H Jones Cres GU11 25 H6
Habershon Dr GU14 15 G3
Hadleigh Gdns GU16 20 C1
Hadleys GU10 36 B5
Hadrians GU9 35 F2
Hagley Rd GU51 16 C5
Haig La GU52 23 F4
Haig Rd GU12 32 A2
Hailsham Cl GU47 6 D2
Haining Gdns GU16 20 D4
Hale Farm Flats*,
Radford Cl GU9 30 D6
Hale Pl GU9 30 D6
Hale Rd GU9 30 D6
Hale Reeds GU9 30 D5
Hale Way GU16 14 A5
Halebourne La GU24 11 H3
Half Moon St GU19 4 C5
Halifax Cl GU14 19 F4
Halimote Rd GU11 31 G2
Hall Cl GU15 8 C5
Hall Farm Cres GU46 3 D3
Hall Grove Fm Ind Est
GU19 4 D3
Hall La GU46 3 C3
Hallgrove Bottom
GU19 4 C3
Hallmark Cl GU47 7 E3
Hamble Av GU17 6 D6
Hambleton Cl GU16 15 E2
Hamesmoor Rd GU16 20 C4
Hamesmoor Way
GU16 20 C3
Hamilton Pl GU11 31 F3
Hamilton Rd GU52 23 F3
Hamlash La GU10 37 F6
Hammersley Rd GU11 25 H3
Hammond Way GU18 10 B2
Hampshire Cl GU12 32 A4
Hampshire Rd GU15 8 C3
Hampton Cl GU32 23 E5
Hampton Rd GU9 30 C4
Hanbury Way GU15 13 H2
Hancombe Rd GU47 6 A1
Handcroft Cl GU10 28 B4
Hanford Cl GU14 3 C3
Hangerfield Cl GU46 3 C3
Hannams Farm Cl
GU10 28 B5
Hanover Cl,
Frimley GU16 14 B4
Hanover Cl,
Yateley GU46 3 D2
Hanover Dr GU51 17 G3
Hanover Gdns GU14 19 E2
Hanson Cl GU15 9 H4
Harbour Cl GU14 13 G5
Harcourt Rd GU15 7 G6
Hardy Av GU46 3 C4
Harlech Rd GU17 12 D1
Harlington Way GU51 22 D1
Harpers Rd GU12 33 F1
Harpton Cl GU46 3 D1
Harpton Par GU46 3 D2
Hart Centre*,
Oakley Pl GU51 17 E6
Hart Cl GU14 13 E5
Hartfield Ho*,
Birch Av GU51 17 E6
Hartford Rise GU15 8 A5
Hartland Pl GU14 19 F1
Hartley Cl GU17 6 B6
Harts Leap Cl GU47 6 A2
Harts Leap Rd GU47 6 A3
Hartsleaf Cl GU51 23 E1
Harvard Rd GU47 7 E1
Harvest Cl GU46 3 B4
Harvest Cres GU51 17 F2
Harvey Rd GU14 18 C2
Haslemere Cl GU16 15 F2
Hastings Cl GU16 20 D1

Hatch End GU20 5 G4
Hatfield Gdns GU14 20 B4
Hatherwood GU46 3 F3
Hatton Hill GU20 5 F2
Haven Way GU9 35 E1
Haweswater Ct*,
Lakeside Cl GU12 26 C5
Hawker Rd GU12 26 C4
Hawkes Leap GU20 5 F2
Hawkesworth GU19 9 G2
Hawkesworth Dr
GU19 9 G2
Hawkins Cl GU46 3 C3
Hawkins Gro GU51 22 C3
Hawkins Way GU52 23 G1
Hawkswood Av GU16 14 C3
Hawkwell GU52 23 F5
Hawley Ct GU14 13 E6
Hawley Gro GU17 13 E3
Hawley La GU14 13 G5
Hawley Rd,
Blackwater GU17 12 D1
Hawley Rd,
Farnborough GU14 13 G5
Hawthorn La GU10 36 C5
Hawthorn Rd GU16 14 C3
Hawthorne Cl GU12 32 B4
Hawthorne Cres GU17 13 E1
Haydon Pl GU46 3 E2
Haywood Dr GU52 23 E2
Hazel Av GU14 19 E5
Hazel Rd, Ash GU12 33 F4
Hazel Rd,
Mytchett GU16 20 D5
Hazeley Dr GU51 16 B4
Hazell Rd GU9 34 A4
Hearmon Cl GU46 3 D2
Hearsey Gdns GU17 6 B5
Heath Cl GU9 30 C4
Heath Cnr GU16 14 D2
Heath Ct*,
Heath Rd GU19 4 C5
Heath La,
Crondall GU10 28 C6
Heath La,
Farnham GU9 30 C4
Heath Pl*,
Heath Rd GU19 4 C5
Heath Rd GU19 4 C5
Heath Rise GU15 8 B6
Heathcote Rd,
Ash GU12 27 E6
Heathcote Rd,
Camberley GU15 8 A6
Heather Cl,
Aldershot GU12 31 E2
Heather Cl, Ash GU12 27 E4
Heather Cl,
Farnham GU9 36 C2
Heather Ct*,
St Josephs Rd GU11 31 G3
Heather Dr GU52 23 E4
Heather Gdns GU14 18 D5
Heather Mead GU16 14 B3
Heather Mead Ct
GU16 14 C3
Heatherdale Rd GU15 14 A1
Heatherley Cl GU15 7 G6
Heatherley Rd GU15 7 G6
Heathfield Cl GU15 22 C2
Heathland St GU11 31 G2
Heathlands Cl GU46 3 E4
Heathpark Dr GU20 5 H4
Heathvale Bridge Rd
GU12 27 E3
Heathway GU15 8 B6
Heathway Cl GU15 8 A6
Heathwood Cl GU46 3 D1
Heathyfields Rd GU9 30 A5
Heckfield Dr GU51 16 B4
Heddon Walk GU14 13 F6
Hedgecroft GU46 3 B2
Heenan Cl GU16 14 B6
Helen Ct GU14 19 G3
Helston Cl GU16 14 D6
Henley Cl GU14 13 E5
Henley Dr GU16 14 B6
Henley Gdns GU46 3 D3
Hepworth Cft GU47 6 D5
Herald Ct GU12 31 G2
Herbert Rd GU15 16 C6
Herbs End GU14 18 C2
Hereford La GU9 30 B5
Hereford Mead GU51 17 F3
Hermes Cl GU51 17 G6
Hermitage Cl,
Farnborough GU14 26 A1
Hermitage Cl,
Frimley GU16 14 C4

Heron Cl,
Church Crookham
GU52 23 G4
Heron Cl,
Mytchett GU16 20 C3
Heron Wood Rd GU12 32 B4
Heronscourt GU18 10 D3
Herrett St GU12 32 A3
Herretts Gdns GU12 32 B3
Herrick Cl GU16 15 F2
Herrings La GU20 5 H3
Herriot Ct GU46 3 C4
Hewlett Pl GU19 4 C4
Hexham Cl GU47 6 D1
Heywood Dr GU19 4 B5
Hicks La GU17 6 B6
Higgs La GU19 4 B5
High Beeches GU16 14 B3
High Copse GU9 30 A5
High Crissels GU47 6 D3
High Park Rd GU9 34 C3
High St,
Aldershot GU11 31 F1
High St, Bagshot GU19 4 B5
High St,
Camberley GU15 8 A5
High St,
Farnborough GU14 26 A1
High St,
Farnham GU10 36 B4
High St,
Sandhurst GU47 6 A2
High St,
Sandhurst GU47 6 A3
High St, Woking GU24 11 F4
High View GU14 19 G3
High View Rd,
Farnborough GU14 19 G3
High View Rd,
Lightwater GU18 10 A3
Highbury Cres GU15 8 D4
Highclere Dr GU15 8 D4
Highclere Rd GU12 32 A3
Highdown GU51 17 E5
Highfield Av GU11 31 G4
Highfield Cl,
Aldershot GU11 31 G3
Highfield Cl,
Farnborough GU14 19 F3
Highfield Cl,
Farnham GU9 34 C6
Highfield Gdns GU11 31 G3
Highfield Path GU14 19 F3
Highfield Rd GU14 19 F3
Highgate La GU14 20 A2
Highgrove GU14 13 H6
Highland Dr GU51 17 G4
Highland Rd,
Aldershot GU12 32 A1
Highland Rd,
Camberley GU15 8 C3
Highlands Cl GU9 37 E1
Highlands Rd GU9 30 C4
Highview Cres GU15 8 C2
Highwaymans Ridge
GU20 5 F2
Highwood Cl GU46 3 C4
Hilder Gdns GU14 20 A4
Hill Crest Dr GU9 36 C2
Hill Rd GU9 30 C4
Hill View Rd GU9 34 A3
Hillary Cl GU9 34 C6
Hillary Rd GU9 34 C6
Hillbrook Rise GU9 30 B5
Hillcrest GU15 17 E4
Hillcrest Rd GU15 9 E3
Hillfield GU46 3 F3
Hillsborough Ct GU14 13 E5
Hillsborough Pk GU14 19 F6
Hillside GU15 7 F4
Hillside Cl GU51 22 A4
Hillside Cotts GU17 13 F4
Hillside Cres GU16 14 C6
Hillside La GU9 30 D4
Hillside Rd,
Aldershot GU11 31 F3
Hillside Rd, Ash GU12 27 E6
Hillside Rd,
Farnham GU10 37 E5
Hillside Rd,
Weybourne GU9 31 E5
Hilltop Vw GU46 3 B3
Hindell Cl GU14 13 G5
Hinstock Rd GU14 19 G4
Hitches La GU13 16 B6
Hodges Cl GU19 9 G2
Hogarth Cl GU47 7 E5
Hoghatch La GU9 30 A5
Hogs Back GU10 33 E6

Holbeche Cl GU46 3
Holbrook Cl GU9 3
Holbrook Way GU11 3
Holder Rd GU12 3
Holland Cl GU9 3
Holland Gdns GU12 3
Hollis Wood Dr GU10 3
Holly Acre GU46 3
Holly Av GU16 1
Holly Bush La GU11 2
Holly Cl,
Aldershot GU12 3
Holly Cl,
Farnborough GU14 1
Holly Hedge Cl GU16 1
Holly Hedge Rd GU16 1
Holly Rd,
Aldershot GU12 3
Holly Rd,
Farnborough GU14 1
Holly Ridge GU24 1
Holly Way GU17 1
Hollybank GU24
Hollybush Ind Pk
GU11
Hollybush Ride GU19
Hollyfields Cl GU9
Hollytree Gdns GU16 1
Hollytrees GU51
Holmbrook Cl GU14 1
Holt Cl GU14 1
Holt Pound La GU10 3
Holywell Cl GU14 2
Home Farm Cl GU14 2
Home Farm Rd RG27
Home Park Dr GU14 1
Homelea Cl GU14 1
Homeleigh Cres GU12 2
Hone Hill GU47
Honeysuckle Cl GU46
Honister Gdns GU51 1
Honister Walk GU15 1
Hook Cl GU47
Hook Mill La GU24
Hookstile La GU9 3
Hookstone La GU24
Hop Gdn GU52
Hope Fountain GU15 1
Hope Grants Rd GU11
Hope La GU24
Hope Way GU11
Hopeman Cl GU47
Hormer Cl GU47
Horn Rd GU14
Hornbeam Cl,
Farnborough GU14
Hornbeam Cl,
Owlsmoor GU47
Hornes Field Ct*,
Annettes Cft GU52
Horsebrass Dr GU19
Horseshoe Cl GU15
Horseshoe Cres GU15
Horseshoe La GU12
Horsham Rd GU47
Hospital Hill GU11
Hospital Rd GU11
Hostel Rd GU14
Houlton Cl GU19
House Plat Ct*,
Annettes Cft GU52
Houseman Rd GU14
Howard Cl GU51 1
Howard Cole Way
GU11
Howard Dr GU14
Howes Gdns GU52
Huddington Glade
GU46
Humber Way GU14
Humphrey Pk GU52
Hungerford Cl GU47
Hunnels Cl GU52
Hunter Rd GU14
Hunters Mws GU11
Hunts La GU15
Huntsmans Mws
GU16
Hurlands Bsns Centre
GU9
Hurlands Cl GU9
Hurlands Pl GU9
Hurst Cl,
Aldershot GU11
Hurst Rd,
Farnborough GU14
Hussar Ct GU11
Hutton Cl GU20
Hutton Rd GU12

le La GU10 | 28 A5
rian Way GU15 | 9 E5
 CI GU46 | 3 B2
n CI GU11 | 31 H1
an Ct GU12 | 31 H3
e Dell GU15 | 14 B1
ewood Av GU15 | 9 F6
sfail Edns GU15 | 31 E3
stitute Rd,
 dershot GU12 | 32 A3
stitute Rd,
 ncible Rd GU14 | 19 F5
ncible Rd Ind Est
 J14 | 19 G5
ne Dr GU14 | 13 E5
Way GU47 | 6 C3
eel La GU10 | 28 A4
y Rd,
 nborough GU14 | 18 C6
y Rd,
 nborough GU14 | 18 D4
 CI GU48 | 3 B1
Dr GU18 | 10 A4
La GU9 | 34 C3
Rd GU12 | 32 B2

ob Rd GU15 | 7 F5
ar Rd GU14 | 19 H5
es Rd,
 dershot GU11 | 26 A2
es Rd,
 mberley GU15 | 13 H3
es Way GU15 | 13 H3
onica Ct GU12 | 32 C2
s Nest CI GU17 | 12 D1
n Orr Ct GU52 | 23 E4
ins Hill GU19 | 4 B6
ner Dr GU14 | 11 G5
ys Walk GU46 | 3 E2
ey CI GU51 | 17 F3
se CI GU46 | 3 F3
sett Dr GU52 | 22 D5
n CI GU11 | 30 D3
nson Way GU52 | 23 E4
lee CI GU14 | 18 C3
lee Ct GU14 | 26 D4
lee Hall Rd GU14 | 19 H3
lee La GU10 | 36 D3
lee Rd,
 dershot GU11 | 31 H4
lee Rd,
 tchett GU16 | 20 D5
ction Rd GU18 | 10 C2
per Rd GU14 | 18 B2

hmir Ct GU14 | 19 H6
ole Rd GU10 | 36 C1
es Gdns GU51 | 23 F1
s Way GU46 | 3 B4
le Way GU47 | 7 E1
 n Lucas Rd GU14 | 19 F5
ey Gro GU46 | 3 E3
Ct GU19 | 4 D6
dal CI GU14 | 18 D4
dal Gro GU15 | 15 G1
lworth Cres GU51 | 17 G5
lworth Rd,
 nborough GU14 | 18 C2
lworth Rd,
 et GU51 | 17 F6
more CI,
 urch Crookham
 52 | 23 F4
more CI,
 ley GU16 | 14 B5
nel La,
 nham GU10 | 37 F5
nel La,
 ndlesham GU20 | 5 F3
nels La GU14 | 18 B4
net CI,
 dershot GU12 | 32 D3
net CI,
 nborough GU14 | 18 D1
sington Ct GU51 | 16 C4
t Rd, Fleet GU51 | 17 F6
t Rd,
 ndlesham GU20 | 5 H3
Co CI GU16 | 14 D3
with Av GU15 | 17 G6
gh CI GU15 | 21 E6
le PI GU19 | 4 C5
ia Way GU24 | 11 F5
y CI GU51 | 17 G2

Kestrel CI GU10 | 29 G4
Kestrel Rd GU14 | 19 H5
Keswick CI GU15 | 15 G1
Keswick Dr GU18 | 10 C3
Kevins Dr GU46 | 3 E2
Kevins Gro GU51 | 17 F6
Keynes CI GU52 | 23 F5
Keynsham Way GU47 | 6 D1
Kielder Walk GU15 | 15 F1
Kilmartin Gdns GU16 | 14 C4
Kilmore Dr GU15 | 15 E1
Kilmuir CI GU47 | 6 D4
Kiln La GU10 | 37 E1
Kiln Way GU11 | 31 G4
Kimberley GU52 | 23 F6
Kimbers La GU9 | 35 E2
Kimpton Dr GU15 | 16 B4
King George CI GU14 | 20 A5
Kingfisher CI,
 Church Crookham
 GU52 | 23 F4
Kingfisher CI,
 Farnborough GU14 | 18 C1
Kingfisher Dr GU46 | 3 B2
Kingfisher Walk GU12 | 32 D1
Kings Av GU10 | 32 C3
Kings Cres GU15 | 8 A3
Kings Ct GU10 | 32 C3
Kings Keep,
 Fleet GU51 | 23 E3
Kings Keep,
 Sandhurst GU47 | 6 B2
Kings La,
 Windlesham GU20 | 5 H3
Kings La,
 Wrecclesham GU9 | 36 C1
Kings Par*,
 Albert St GU51 | 17 E6
Kings Rd,
 Aldershot GU11 | 31 E2
Kings Rd, Fleet GU51 | 17 E5
Kings Rd,
 West End GU24 | 11 G6
Kings Ride GU15 | 8 A2
Kings Walk GU15 | 7 F5
Kingsclear Pk GU15 | 14 A1
Kingscroft GU51 | 23 E1
Kingsley Av GU15 | 14 A1
Kingsley Rd GU14 | 19 F1
Kingsley Sq GU51 | 16 A4
Kingsmead,
 Camberley GU16 | 20 C1
Kingsmead,
 Farnborough GU14 | 19 H3
Kingston Rd GU15 | 8 D3
Kingstons Ind Est
 GU12 | 32 B1
Kingsway,
 Aldershot GU11 | 31 E2
Kingsway,
 Camberley GU17 | 6 D6
Kingswood Ct*,
 Kings Wood GU17 | 17 F6
Kingsworthy Rd GU51 | 16 A4
Kipling CI GU46 | 3 C4
Kirkham CI GU47 | 6 D1
Kirkstone CI GU15 | 15 G1
Kirriemuir Gdns GU12 | 23 F6
Kitcheners Rd GU11 | 26 A3
Knights Rd GU9 | 30 D5
Knightsbridge Gro
 GU15 | 8 B4
Knightsbridge Rd GU15 | 8 B4
Knoll CI GU51 | 17 E5
Knoll Ct GU51 | 17 E4
Knoll Rd,
 Camberley GU15 | 8 A5
Knoll Rd, Fleet GU51 | 17 E5
Knoll Walk GU15 | 8 A5
Knollys Rd GU11 | 25 F6
Knox CI GU52 | 22 C4
Kohat Ct GU11 | 31 E2
Kohima CI GU11 | 31 H1
Krooner Rd GU15 | 13 H2

Laburnum CI GU11 | 31 F2
Laburnum Gdns GU52 | 23 F5
Laburnum Rd GU11 | 31 F2
Ladywood Av GU14 | 18 C3
Ladywood Ct GU10 | 36 D3
Laffans Rd GU11 | 24 C3
Laird Ct GU19 | 9 H1
Lake Rd GU16 | 20 D1
Lakeland Dr GU14 | 14 C4
Lakeside Bsns Pk
 GU47 | 6 A4
Lakeside CI GU12 | 26 C5
Lakeside CI GU51 | 17 F4
Lakeside Gdns GU14 | 12 D6

Lakeside Rd,
 Ash Vale GU12 | 26 C5
Lakeside Rd,
 Farnborough GU14 | 25 F2
Lambert Cres GU17 | 12 C1
Lamborne CI GU47 | 6 A2
Lambourne Dr GU19 | 4 B6
Lambourne Way
 GU10 | 32 C5
Lanark CI GU16 | 14 C3
Lancaster Av GU10 | 34 D5
Lancaster CI GU12 | 26 D5
Lancaster Dr GU15 | 8 B5
Lancaster Rd GU14 | 19 H6
Lancaster Way GU14 | 13 H6
Lancer Ct GU11 | 31 E2
Landseer CI GU47 | 7 E5
Langdale CI GU14 | 19 E3
Langdale Ct*,
 Lakeside Rd GU12 | 26 C5
Langdon CI GU15 | 15 F1
Langham Ct GU9 | 34 D6
Langley CI GU52 | 22 D5
Langley Dr,
 Aldershot GU11 | 31 C3
Langley Dr,
 Camberley GU15 | 8 B5
Lansdowne Rd,
 Aldershot GU11 | 31 F2
Lansdowne Rd,
 Frimley GU16 | 14 D5
Larch CI GU15 | 8 C2
Larch Way GU14 | 18 C4
Larches Way GU17 | 6 B6
Larchfield Rd GU52 | 23 F2
Larchwood Glade
 GU15 | 8 D4
Larkfield CI GU9 | 34 A3
Larkfield Rd GU9 | 34 A3
Larkspur CI GU11 | 31 G4
Larkswood CI GU47 | 6 A2
Larmer CI GU51 | 22 C2
Lashad Rd GU51 | 16 B4
Latchwood La GU10 | 37 G3
Latham Av GU16 | 14 B4
Lauder CI GU16 | 14 B3
Laundry La GU47 | 7 E5
Laurel CI,
 Camberley GU15 | 14 A1
Laurel CI,
 Farnborough GU14 | 18 C4
Laurel Gdns GU11 | 31 G4
Laurel Gro GU10 | 36 C3
Lavender La GU10 | 36 C3
Laverdale GU14 | 18 D5
Lawday Link GU9 | 30 A5
Lawday PI La GU9 | 30 A5
Lawford Cres GU46 | 3 D2
Lawrence Cres GU20 | 5 G4
Lawrence Rd GU52 | 22 D2
Lawrence Way GU15 | 13 F1
Laws Ter GU11 | 31 H1
Le Borowe GU52 | 22 C6
Le Marchant Heights
 GU15 | 14 C2
Le Marchant Rd GU15 | 14 C2
Lea CI, Ash GU12 | 33 E2
Lea CI,
 Badshot Lea GU9 | 31 G5
Lea Rd GU15 | 31 F4
Lea Rd GU15 | 13 G3
Lea Springs GU51 | 22 C2
Lea Way GU12 | 26 C6
Leawood Rd GU51 | 22 C2
Ledger CI GU52 | 22 C5
Lee CI GU11 | 31 H3
Lee Rd GU11 | 30 D2
Lefroy Pk GU51 | 16 D6
Lefroys Fld GU10 | 28 B4
Legge Cres GU11 | 31 E2
Leigh La GU9 | 35 F6
Leipzig Rd GU52 | 23 F6
Leith Dr GU11 | 31 F1
Lendore Rd GU16 | 14 A5
Lennel Gdns GU52 | 23 G3
Leonard CI GU16 | 14 A5
Leopold Av GU14 | 19 G2
Lestock Way GU51 | 17 G6
Levern Dr GU9 | 30 C5
Levignen CI GU52 | 22 C4
Lewisham Way GU47 | 6 D1
Ley Rd GU14 | 13 G5
Leycester CI GU20 | 5 F2
Lichfield Dr GU15 | 16 B4
Lickfolds Rd GU10 | 36 B5
Lightwater Mdw GU18 | 10 C3
Lightwater Rd GU18 | 10 C3
Lime Av GU15 | 8 D5

Lime Cres GU12 | 33 E2
Lime St GU11 | 31 F2
Limecroft GU46 | 3 C3
Limes Rd GU14 | 18 C2
Lincoln CI,
 Ash Vale GU12 | 26 D4
Lincoln CI,
 Camberley GU15 | 15 E1
Linden Ct GU15 | 8 C4
Lindum CI GU11 | 31 G3
Lindum Dene GU11 | 31 F3
Ling Dr GU18 | 10 A4
Lingmala Gro GU52 | 23 F5
Links Way GU14 | 18 C4
Linkway,
 Camberley GU15 | 14 A2
Linkway, Fleet GU52 | 23 E3
Linkway Par GU52 | 23 E3
Linsford Bsns Pk
 GU16 | 20 C4
Linsford La GU16 | 20 C4
Linstead Rd GU14 | 13 E5
Lion and Lamb Way
 GU9 | 34 C3
Lion and Lamb Yd
 GU9 | 34 C3
Lion Rd GU14 | 19 H5
Lion Way GU52 | 23 G5
Lisa Dr GU51 | 16 B4
Liskeard Dr GU14 | 19 F1
Lismoyne CI GU51 | 16 D5
Little Austins Rd GU9 | 35 E5
Little Cft GU46 | 3 D4
Little Copse,
 Fleet GU52 | 23 E2
Little Copse,
 Yateley GU46 | 3 D1
Little Green La GU9 | 36 D1
Little Moor GU47 | 6 B2
Little Pad GU15 | 9 E3
Little Thurbans CI GU9 | 36 D1
Little Vigo GU46 | 3 B4
Little Wellington St
 GU11 | 31 G1
Littlefield CI GU12 | 32 D2
Littlefield Gdns GU12 | 32 D2
Lock Rd GU11 | 26 B4
Lockwood CI GU14 | 13 E5
Loddon CI GU15 | 9 E5
Loddon Rd GU14 | 18 D1
Loddon Way GU12 | 32 D3
Lodge CI GU11 | 31 H3
Lodge Gro GU46 | 3 F2
Lodge Hill CI GU10 | 37 G1
Lodge Hill Rd GU10 | 37 G1
Lodsworth GU14 | 18 D4
Loman Rd GU16 | 20 D4
Londlandes GU52 | 22 C5
London Rd,
 Bagshot GU19 | 4 B5
London Rd,
 Blackwater GU17 | 12 A2
London Rd,
 Camberley GU15 | 7 F6
London Rd,
 Windlesham GU20 | 5 E2
Lone Acre GU20 | 5 H4
Long Beech Dr GU14 | 18 C4
Long Bridge GU9 | 34 D4
Long Garden PI*,
 Long Garden Walk
 GU9 | 34 C3
Long Garden Walk
 GU9 | 34 C3
Long Garden Way
 GU9 | 34 C3
Long Mickle GU47 | 6 A2
Long Sutton Dr GU51 | 16 B4
Longacre GU12 | 32 D1
Longdown GU52 | 22 D3
Longdown CI GU10 | 37 F2
Longdown Rd,
 Farnham GU10 | 37 E3
Longdown Rd,
 Sandhurst GU47 | 6 A2
Longfield CI GU14 | 13 G5
Longfield Rd GU12 | 32 D2
Longford CI GU15 | 14 B1
Longhope Dr GU10 | 36 D2
Longlands Way GU15 | 9 G6
Longleat Sq GU14 | 20 B4
Longley Rd GU9 | 35 E4
Longmead GU52 | 23 E3
Longmeadow GU16 | 14 C2
Longmoor Ct GU51 | 16 B4
Lorraine Rd GU15 | 8 C3
Lory Ridge GU19 | 4 C4
Louise Margaret Rd
 GU11 | 25 H6

Love La, Ash GU12 | 33 E1
Love La, Yateley GU46 | 3 A2
Lovells CI GU18 | 10 C2
Low La GU9 | 31 G5
Lowa La GU11 | 25 E6
Lower Canes GU46 | 3 A2
Lower Charles St
 GU15 | 7 H5
Lower Church La GU14 | 34 C4
Lower Farnham Rd
 GU11,12 | 31 H5
Lower Gordon Rd
 GU15 | 13 H1
Lower Mill Fld GU19 | 4 B6
Lower Moor GU46 | 3 D3
Lower Mount St GU51 | 16 B4
Lower Nelson St
 GU11 | 31 G1
Lower Newport Rd
 GU12 | 32 B3
Lower South Vw GU9 | 34 D3
Lower Weybourne La
 GU9 | 31 E5
Loweswater Walk
 GU15 | 15 G1
Lowfield CI GU18 | 10 B3
Lowlands Rd GU17 | 12 C1
Lowndes Bldgs GU9 | 34 C3
Lowry CI GU47 | 6 D5
Loxwood Av GU51 | 22 C3
Lucas CI GU46 | 3 D3
Lucas Green Rd GU24 | 11 G5
Ludlow CI GU16 | 14 D6
Luke Rd GU11 | 31 E3
Luke Rd East GU11 | 31 E3
Lulworth CI GU14 | 13 G6
Lupin CI GU19 | 9 F2
Lyall PI GU9 | 30 B4
Lydford CI,
 Farnborough GU14 | 13 F6
Lydford CI,
 Frimley Green GU16 | 14 D6
Lye Copse Av GU14 | 13 G5
Lymington Av GU46 | 3 C3
Lynams GU52 | 22 C6
Lynch Rd GU9 | 35 E4
Lynchford La GU14 | 26 C1
Lynchford Rd GU11 | 25 H2
Lyndale Dr GU51 | 17 H6
Lyndford Ter GU52 | 23 E2
Lyndhurst Av,
 Aldershot GU11 | 31 H5
Lyndhurst Av,
 Blackwater GU17 | 6 C5
Lyndhurst Rd GU51 | 16 B4
Lyndsey CI GU14 | 18 B3
Lynn Way GU14 | 13 E6
Lynton CI GU9 | 34 B6
Lynwood Dr GU16 | 20 D4
Lyon Way GU16 | 13 H4
Lyon Way Ind Est
 GU16 | 14 A4
Lysander Way GU14 | 19 H6
Lysons Av GU12 | 26 C1
Lysons Rd GU11 | 31 F2
Lysons Way GU12 | 26 D2

Macdonald Rd,
 Farnham GU9 | 30 B4
Macdonald Rd,
 Lightwater GU18 | 10 A3
MacNaughten Woods
 GU15 | 8 B5
Macrae Rd GU14 | 3 C2
Madeley Rd GU52 | 23 F3
Madox Brown End
 GU47 | 6 D4
Magdalene Rd GU47 | 7 E1
Magnolia CI GU47 | 6 D2
Magnolia Way GU52 | 23 E2
Magpie CI GU10 | 29 G4
Maguire Dr GU16 | 15 F2
Mahonia CI GU24 | 11 F5
Maida Rd GU11 | 25 G6
Main Gate Rd GU14 | 19 G5
Mainstone CI GU14 | 15 F6
Maitland CI GU14 | 25 H1
Maitlands CI GU10 | 32 C5
Mallard CI GU12 | 32 D1
Mallard Way GU46 | 3 B3
Mallards Way GU18 | 10 A3
Malta Rd GU16 | 15 G5
Malthouse CI GU52 | 22 C4
Malthouse La GU24 | 11 G5
Malvern Rd GU14 | 12 D6
Mandarin Ct*,
 Radford GU9 | 30 D6
Mandora Rd GU11 | 25 H6
Manfield Rd GU12 | 32 D2

Manley Bridge Rd GU10 36 B4
Manor Cl GU10 32 C4
Manor Ct GU52 23 E5
Manor Farm Cl GU12 32 C3
Manor Gdns GU10 37 G3
Manor Park Dr GU46 3 D3
Manor Pk Ind Est GU12 31 H2
Manor Rd, Aldershot GU11 31 F3
Manor Rd, Farnborough GU14 20 B4
Manor Rd, Farnham GU9 35 E1
Manor Rd, Tongham GU10 32 C4
Manor Walk GU12 31 H2
Manor Way GU19 4 C6
Manorside Cl GU10 32 C3
Maple Cl, Ash Vale GU12 26 D2
Maple Cl, Blackwater GU17 6 C6
Maple Dr GU18 10 A3
Maple Gdns GU46 3 D3
Maple Leaf Cl GU14 19 F4
Maple Walk GU12 32 B4
Mardale GU15 15 F1
Mareth Cl GU11 31 H1
Mariners Dr GU14 20 A1
Marjoram Cl GU14 18 B3
Markham Ct GU15 8 B5
Marlborough Cl GU51 23 H1
Marlborough Rise GU15 8 C5
Marlborough Vw GU14 18 C2
Marrowbrook Cl GU14 19 F4
Marrowbrook La GU14 19 F5
Marshall Cl, Camberley GU16 15 G3
Marshall Cl, Farnborough GU14 13 E6
Marshall Rd GU47 6 D5
Marshwood Rd GU18 10 D2
Marston Dr GU14 13 H6
Marston Rd GU9 34 A4
Martel Cl GU15 9 F4
Martin Way GU16 14 B4
Martindale Av GU15 15 F2
Martingale Ct GU11 31 H2
Martins Ct GU17 12 C1
Marwell Rd GU51 16 B4
Maskell Way GU14 18 C4
Mason Cl GU46 3 E3
Mason Rd GU14 19 E1
Mason Way GU11 31 G4
Mathews Cl GU14 26 B1
Mathews Ter GU11 31 G4
Matthew Rd GU11 30 D3
Matthews Rd GU15 8 A3
Maultway Cl GU15 9 E3
Maultway Cres GU15 9 E3
Maultway North GU15 9 E2
Mavins Rd GU9 35 E5
Maxine Cl GU47 6 D2
May Cl GU47 6 D2
May Cres GU12 32 C2
Maybury Cl GU16 14 A5
Mayfair Ct GU51 16 C4
Mayfield GU10 36 C4
Mayfield GU18 31 G5
Mayfield Rd, Camberley GU15 13 H4
Mayfield Rd, Farnborough GU14 13 E6
Mayflower Dr GU46 3 A1
Maywood Dr GU15 9 E4
McKay Cl GU12 32 A1
McNaughton Cl GU14 18 C4
Mead La GU9 34 C4
Meade Ct GU19 4 D5
Meadow Bank GU9 34 C4
Meadow Cl, Ash Vale GU12 26 C1
Meadow Cl, Blackwater GU17 12 D1
Meadow Cotts GU24 11 F5
Meadow Ct, Farnborough GU14 19 F3
Meadow Ct, Fleet GU51 16 D6
Meadow Gate Av GU14 19 F6
Meadow Rd GU14 13 G6
Meadow Vw GU52 22 C4
Meadow Walk GU51 22 C2

Meadow Way, Aldershot GU12 32 C1
Meadow Way, Blackwater GU17 6 C6
Meadow Way, Rowledge GU10 36 C4
Meadow Way, West End GU24 11 F4
Meadowbank Rd GU18 10 D2
Meadway GU16 14 C3
Medlar Dr GU17 13 F2
Medonte Cl GU18 13 E6
Medstead Dr GU51 16 B4
Medway Dr GU14 13 E6
Melksham Cl GU47 6 D1
Mellersh Cl GU52 22 D5
Melrose Av GU14 18 C3
Melville Av GU16 14 C4
Membury Cl GU16 14 D6
Mendip Rd GU14 13 E6
Menin Way GU9 35 E5
Meon Cl GU11 18 D1
Merivale GU51 22 C1
Merlin Ct GU16 14 A4
Merlin Rd GU14 19 H5
Merlin Way GU14 18 D4
Merlins Cl GU9 34 D5
Merron Cl GU46 3 C3
Merrywood Pk GU15 14 C1
Merryworth Cl GU12 32 C3
Merton Cl GU47 7 E1
Meudon Av GU14 19 G4
Michaelmas Cl GU46 3 D4
Micheldever Dr GU51 16 B4
Michelet Cl GU18 10 C2
Mickle Hill GU47 6 A2
Middle Av GU9 35 E6
Middle Bourne La GU10 37 E1
Middle Church La GU9 34 C3
Middle Cl GU15 9 F5
Middle Gordon Rd GU15 8 A6
Middle Hill GU11 25 G6
Middle Oak Pk GU9 34 A1
Middlefield GU9 34 B6
Middlefield Cl GU9 34 B6
Middlemoor Cl GU16 14 C5
Middlemoor Rd GU16 14 B5
Middleton Gdns GU14 19 E1
Middleton Rd GU15 8 C5
Mike Hawthorn Dr GU9 34 D3
Milden Cl GU16 20 D1
Milden Gdns GU16 20 D1
Miles Pl GU18 10 A4
Miles Rd GU12 33 E1
Mill Cnr GU51 17 G3
Mill Fld GU19 4 B5
Mill La GU46 3 D1
Mill Pond Rd GU20 5 F2
Millbridge Rd GU46 3 B1
Millgate Ct GU9 35 E7
Millholme Walk GU15 15 F1
Millins Cl GU47 6 D2
Millmere GU46 3 D1
Millstream GU19 31 E5
Milney Rd GU14 19 E3
Milton Grange GU12 27 E5
Minehurst Rd GU16 20 C3
Minerva Rd GU14 19 H6
Minley Cl GU14 19 E3
Minley Gro GU51 17 F4
Minley Rd, Farnborough GU14 12 A6
Minley Rd, Fleet GU51 17 F3
Minorca Av GU16 15 H4
Minorca Rd GU16 15 H4
Minstead Dr GU46 3 C3
Minster Ct, Camberley GU15 7 F6
Minster Ct, Camberley GU15 8 A4
Mistletoe Rd GU46 3 D4
Mitcham Rd GU15 8 A2
Moffatts Cl GU47 6 A3
Mole Cl GU14 19 E1
Molyneux Rd GU20 5 G4
Monks Cl GU14 19 H3
Monks Rise GU51 22 C1
Monks Walk GU9 35 G6
Monkshanger GU9 35 F3
Monkton Cl GU9 30 D6
Monkton Pk GU9 35 G1
Mons Cl GU15 26 B3
Montacute Cl GU14 20 B3

Montague Cl, Camberley GU15 7 G6
Montague Cl, Lightwater GU18 10 B2
Monteagle La GU46 3 A3
Montgomery Cl GU47 6 B3
Montgomery Rd GU14 19 F4
Montrose Cl, Fleet GU51 23 F1
Montrose Cl, Frimley GU16 14 B3
Moons Hill GU10 37 E5
Moor Cl GU47 7 E2
Moor Park La GU9 35 F2
Moor Park Way GU9 35 G4
Moor Pl GU20 5 F3
Moor Rd, Farnborough GU14 13 G5
Moor Rd, Frimley Green GU16 14 C6
Moore Cl, Aldershot GU12 32 C2
Moore Cl, Fleet GU52 23 F4
Moore Rd GU52 23 F4
Moorlands Cl GU51 23 F1
Moorlands Pl GU15 7 G6
Moorlands Rd GU15 13 G1
Moorside Cl GU14 13 F5
Moray Av GU47 6 D4
Moreton Cl GU52 22 D5
Morland Rd GU11 31 H5
Morlands Rd GU11 26 A4
Morley Cl GU46 3 A3
Morley Rd GU9 34 D5
Morris Rd GU14 26 B1
Morton Cl GU16 14 C6
Morval Cl GU14 18 D3
Moselle Cl GU14 18 D2
Moulsham Copse La GU46 3 B1
Moulsham La GU46 3 B1
Mount Pleasant, Farnham GU9 34 B4
Mount Pleasant, Sandhurst GU47 6 A1
Mount Pleasant Cl GU18 10 B2
Mount Pleasant Rd GU12 31 H2
Mount Vw GU11 31 F3
Mountbatten Ct*, Fir Tree All GU11 31 G1
Mounts Way GU51 16 B4
Mulberry Cl, Ash GU12 27 E5
Mulberry Cl, Owlsmoor GU47 6 D3
Mulgrave Rd GU16 14 C3
Mulroy Dr GU15 9 E5
Munnings Dr GU47 6 D5
Murray Rd GU14 19 F4
Murrays Rd GU11 26 A4
Murrell Rd GU12 33 E1
Murrells La GU15 13 H2
Myers Way GU16 15 G3
Myrtle Cl GU18 10 C3
Myrtle Dr GU17 6 D6
Mytchett Heath GU16 20 D5
Mytchett Lake Rd GU16 20 D6
Mytchett Place Rd GU16 20 D5
Mytchett Rd GU16 20 C3

Nairn Cl GU16 14 B3
Napier Cl GU11 26 B2
Napier Dr GU15 8 D4
Napier La GU15 26 D5
Napoleon Av GU14 19 H2
Nash Cl GU14 19 E3
Neelem Ct GU14 25 H1
Nelson Cl, Aldershot GU12 32 A2
Nelson Cl, Farnham GU9 30 D3
Nelson Rd GU9 30 D4
Nelson St GU11 31 F1
Nelson Way GU15 13 E1
Nether Vell-Mead GU52 22 D6
Netherhouse Ct GU52 22 C3
Netherhouse Moor GU51 22 C2
Netley St GU14 25 H1
Nevada Cl GU14 18 D4
Neville Duke Rd GU14 13 F5
New Barn Cl GU51 22 C2
New Dawn Cl GU14 18 D4

New Rd, Bagshot GU19 4 D5
New Rd, Blackwater GU17 13 E1
New Rd, Church Crookham GU52 23 F3
New Rd, Sandhurst GU47 6 A3
New Rd, Tongham GU10 32 C5
New Rd, Windlesham GU20 5 F4
Newark Rd GU20 5 F1
Newcome Pl GU12 32 A4
Newcome Rd GU9 31 E5
Newfield Av GU14 19 E1
Newfield Rd GU12 26 D3
Newfoundland Rd GU16 15 G5
Newlands GU52 23 E3
Newlands Cl GU46 3 D4
Newlands Dr GU12 27 E5
Newlands Rd GU15 13 H4
Newmans Ct GU9 30 A5
Newport Rd GU12 31 H2
Newton Rd GU14 20 A1
Newton Way GU10 32 C4
Newtown Rd GU47 6 A3
Nexus Pk GU12 26 D2
Nicotiana Ct*, Annettes Cft GU52 22 D5
Nightingale Cl GU15 18 C1
Nightingale Dr GU16 20 D4
Nightingale Gdns GU47 6 B3
Nightingale Rd GU12 27 F6
Nightjar Cl GU10 29 F3
Norman Ct GU9 34 D4
Normandy Cl GU16 15 H5
Norris Hill Rd GU51 23 G1
North Av GU9 30 D5
North Cl, Aldershot GU12 32 B3
North Cl, Farnborough GU14 13 G5
North Farm Rd GU14 13 E5
North Fryerne GU46 3 D1
North Gate Rd GU19 19 H5
North La GU12 26 A6
North Mall GU51 17 E6
North Rd, Ash GU12 26 D5
North Side GU10 32 C5
Northbrook Rd GU11 31 G3
Northcote Rd, Ash Vale GU12 26 D3
Northcote Rd, Farnborough GU14 19 E1
Northdown Trading Est GU12 32 B2
Northfield GU18 10 C3
Northfield Cl, Aldershot GU12 32 B2
Northfield Cl, Church Crookham GU52 23 G4
Northfield Rd GU52 23 G4
Northgate Dr GU15 8 D4
Northmead GU14 19 G4
Norton Rd GU15 15 F1
Norwich Av GU15 14 B2
Nuffield Dr GU47 7 E2
Nursery Cl, Fleet GU51 23 H1
Nursery Cl, Frimley Green GU16 20 C1
Nutbourne GU9 31 E4
Nutfield Ct GU15 8 A4
Nuthatch Cl GU10 29 F4
Nutley Cl GU46 3 D3
Nutley Dr GU51 16 B4
Nutmeg Cl GU14 18 C2
Nutshell La GU9 30 C5

Oak Av GU47 6 D2
Oak Cl GU14 18 C4
Oak Ct, Farnborough GU14 20 B6
Oak Ct, Farnham GU9 34 C5
Oak Farm Cl GU17 6 C6
Oak Grove Cres GU15 7 E5
Oak Rd GU14 19 H4
Oak Tree Cl, Aldershot GU12 32 B4
Oak Tree Cl, Ash Vale GU12 26 D1
Oak Tree Vw GU9 30 D6

Oak Tree Way GU47 6
Oaken Copse GU52 23
Oaken Copse Cres GU14 13
Oakfield Rd GU17 13
Oakhanger Ho GU51 16
Oakland Av GU9 31
Oaklands GU46 3
Oaklea GU12 26
Oakleigh GU18 10
Oakley Dr GU51 23
Oakley Pl GU51 17
Oakley Rd GU15 13
Oakridge GU24 11
Oaktrees, Ash GU12 32
Oaktrees, Farnham GU9 30
Oakway GU12 32
Oakway Dr GU16 14
Oakwood GU52 23
Oakwood Rd GU20 5
Oast House Cres GU9 30
Oast La GU11 31
Oasthouse Dr GU51 17
Obelisk Way GU11 31
Oberursel Way GU11 31
Observer Cl GU52 22
O'Connor Rd GU11 26
Odiham Rd GU10 29
O'Gorman Av GU14 19
Okingham Cl GU47 6
Old Bisley Rd GU16 14
Old Brickfield Rd GU11 31
Old Chapel La GU12 32
Old Church La GU9 35
Old Compton La GU9 35
Old Cove Rd GU51 17
Old Cross Tree Way GU12 33
Old Dean Rd GU15 8
Old Farm Pl GU12 26
Old Farnham La GU9 34
Old Forge End GU47 6
Old Frensham Rd GU10 37
Old Green La GU15 9
Old Guildford Rd GU16 21
Old Heath Way GU9 30
Old La, Aldershot GU11 31
Old La, North Town GU12 32
Old Mills Par GU47 6
Old Park Cl GU9 30
Old Park La, Farnham GU9 29
Old Park La, Farnham GU9 30
Old Pasture Rd GU16 14
Old Pond Cl GU15 13
Old Portsmouth Rd GU15 8
Old Pumpho Cl GU51 17
Old Rectory Dr GU12 33
Old Rectory Gdns GU14 20
Old School Cl, Ash GU12 27
Old School Cl, Fleet GU51 17
Old School La GU46 3
Old Welmore GU46 3
Oldacre GU24 11
Oldbury Cl GU14 14
Oldcorne Hollow GU46 3
Olde Farm Dr GU17 6
Oldhouse La, Bisley GU24 11
Oldhouse La, Windlesham GU20
Oldwood Chase GU14 18
Orchard Cl, Ash Vale GU12 26
Orchard Cl, Badshot Lea GU9 31
Orchard Cl, Blackwater GU17 13
Orchard Cl, West End GU24 11
Orchard End GU10 28
Orchard End GU10 28
Orchard Flds GU51 16
Orchard Gate GU47 6
Orchard Gdns GU12 33
Orchard Hill GU20 5
Orchard Mws GU18 10

hard Rd,
dshot Lea GU9 31 G5
hard Rd,
rnborough GU14 19 G3
hard Way,
dershot GU12 32 A4
hard Way,
mberley GU15 13 G3
nance Rd GU11 26 A6
el Hill GU15 14 A1
vell Cl GU14 19 E1
orn Rd GU9 35 E1
orne Cl GU16 14 C5
orne Dr GU18 10 B3
orne Rd GU52 23 F2
ourne Ct GU14 25 H1
ourne GU14 25 H1
aburgh Hill GU15 7 G6
rdale Rise GU16 14 B2
rlord Cl GU15 7 H3
rton Cl GU11 31 H5
gton Dr GU51 16 B4
en Rd GU20 5 H3
smoor Rd GU24 6 D3
nden Ct GU10 32 C4
nden Rd GU10 32 C3
ord Rd,
rnborough GU14 20 A6
ord Rd,
dhurst GU47 7 E1
kway GU9 35 E6
dock Cl GU15 8 D5
et Cl GU15 9 E4
enham Dr GU11 31 F1
La, Hook RG27 16 A3
La, Hook RG27 16 A4
nerston Cl GU14 18 D4
per Dr GU51 16 B4
kridge St GU10 28 B3
ells GU10 37 G2
s Gdns GU15 14 C1
itts Cl GU9 34 B4
sh Cl, Ash GU12 33 E2
sh Cl,
nham GU9 30 A5
sh Rd GU14 25 H1
Av GU15 14 A1
k Fm Ind Est
J16 13 H4
Hill GU52 23 E5
La GU15 8 A6
Pl GU52 23 E5
Rd,
dershot GU11 31 H4
Rd,
mberley GU15 13 H2
Rd,
rnborough GU14 20 B6
Rd,
nham GU9 35 E2
Rd,
dhurst GU47 6 C4
Row GU9 34 C3
St, Bagshot GU19 4 C5
St,
mberley GU15 8 A5
Vw GU19 4 B5
ers Cl GU9 4 C5
fields GU46 3 D3
idge Cl,
12 D1
hill Rd GU17 12 D1
land Gro GU9 31 F4
side GU9 30 C5
stone Dr GU15 13 H1
way GU15 13 H2
ham Av GU18 10 D3
onage Way GU16 14 B5
ons Cl GU52 23 E4
ons Fld GU47 6 B3
idge Av GU46 3 B2
idge Cl,
idge Cl,
mley GU16 14 B4
hal GU15 8 D3
en Av GU46 3 C3
erson Cl GU14 15 F2
Cl GU11 31 E3
lion Rd GU11 31 E2
lion Ter GU11 27 E6
mers Mead GU52 22 C6
ody Rd GU14 26 A1
ch Tree Cl GU14 13 G6
Tree La GU10 36 C5
tree Cotts GU14 18 C5
moor Cl GU51 16 D5
dlars Gro GU46 3 E2
GU16 14 D6

Peel Ct GU14 25 H2
Pegasus Av GU12 32 A5
Pegasus Ct GU14 20 B6
Pegasus Ct*,
Birch Av GU51 17 E6
Pegasus Rd GU14 13 F6
Peggotty Pl GU47 7 E1
Pelham Pl GU10 36 D3
Pembroke Broadway
GU15 8 A6
Pembroke Par GU46 3 E2
Pembury Pl GU12 31 H2
Pendragon Way GU15 15 G1
Penfold Cft GU9 35 H2
Pengilly Rd GU9 34 C4
Peninsula Cl GU15 9 E4
Pennefathers Rd GU11 25 F6
Pennine Way GU14 12 D6
Penns Wood GU14 20 A6
Pennypot La GU24 11 H5
Penrhyn Cl GU11 31 G3
Penshurst Rise GU16 14 D5
Pentland Pl GU14 12 D6
Perowne St GU11 31 F1
Perring Av GU15 13 E5
Perry Cl GU12 26 C5
Perry Dr GU13 16 B6
Perry Way GU18 10 A4
Peterhouse Cl GU47 7 E1
Petworth Cl GU16 14 C1
Petworth Cl GU15 14 C1
Pevensey Way GU16 14 D5
Pheasant Copse GU51 16 C5
Phoenix Cl GU11 31 G2
Pickford St GU11 31 G2
Pickwick Gdns GU15 15 E1
Picton Cl GU15 9 E4
Pierrefondes Av GU14 19 G2
Pike Cl GU12 32 A1
Pilcot Rd GU51 16 A3
Pilgrims Cl GU9 34 B5
Pilgrims Vw GU12 33 F4
Pine Av GU15 14 A1
Pine Cl,
Aldershot GU12 26 D3
Pine Cl,
Sandhurst GU47 7 E4
Pine Dr GU17 13 E2
Pine Gro,
Church Crookham
GU52 23 F4
Pine Gro,
Lower Bourne GU10 37 G1
Pine Gro,
Windlesham GU20 5 H4
Pine Mount Rd GU15 14 B1
Pine Ridge Dr GU10 37 E2
Pine View Cl GU9 31 F6
Pinehill Rise GU47 16 B4
Pinehurst Av GU14 19 G5
Pinehurst Cotts GU14 19 G5
Pines Rd GU51 16 D5
Pineview GU14 19 F4
Pinewood Cl GU47 3 F1
Pinewood Cres GU14 18 C2
Pinewood Cl*,
Pinewood Hill GU51 17 E6
Pinewood Gdns GU19 4 A5
Pinewood Hill GU51 17 E6
Pinewood Pk GU14 12 C6
Pinewood Rd GU12 27 G6
Pipers Cft GU52 23 E5
Pipers Patch GU14 19 H3
Pipsons Cl GU46 3 D2
Pirbright Rd,
Farnborough GU14 20 A5
Pirbright Rd,
Normandy GU3 27 H6
Pitt Way GU14 19 F2
Place Ct GU11 32 A5
Plantation Row GU15 7 G6
Plough Rd GU46 3 E2
Polden Cl GU14 13 E6
Polkerris Way GU52 23 G5
Pollard Gro GU14 15 F1
Polmear Cl GU52 23 F5
Pond Cft GU46 3 E2
Pond Rd GU14 19 H5
Pond View Cl GU51 17 G5
Pondtail Cl GU51 23 G1
Pondtail Gdns GU51 23 G1
Pondtail Rd GU51 23 G1
Pool Rd GU11 32 A5
Poplar Av GU20 5 E2
Poplar Cl,
Farnborough GU14 18 C2
Poplar Cl,
Mytchett GU16 20 D4
Poplar Walk GU9 30 D5

Poppyhills Rd GU15 8 C3
Portesbery Hill Dr GU15 8 B4
Portesbery Rd GU15 8 B5
Portland Dr GU52 23 E5
Portsmouth Rd,
Camberley GU15 8 D5
Portsmouth Rd,
Frimley GU15,16 14 A4
Potley Hill Rd GU46 3 F3
Potteries La GU16 20 C4
Potters Cres GU14 33 E1
Potters Gate GU9 34 B5
Potters Ind Pk GU52 23 G4
Pottery Ct GU10 36 C2
Pottery La GU10 36 C2
Pound Farm La GU12 33 G2
Pound La GU20 5 G4
Pound Rd GU12 31 H2
Poyle Rd GU10 32 C5
Prentice Cl GU14 13 G5
Preymead Ind Est
GU9 31 G5
Priest La GU24 10 D5
Primrose Gdns GU14 19 E4
Primrose Walk GU46 3 B2
Primrose Walk*,
Stockton Pk GU51 17 E5
Primrose Way GU47 6 B2
Prince Charles Cres
GU14 13 F6
Prince Ct GU52 23 E3
Prince Dr GU47 6 A2
Prince of Wales Walk*,
Bietigheim Way GU15 8 A5
Princes Av GU11 25 H4
Princes Way,
Aldershot GU11 31 F1
Princes Way,
Bagshot GU19 9 H1
Princess Way GU15 8 A4
Prior Croft Cl GU15 15 E1
Prior End GU15 8 D6
Prior Rd GU15 8 D6
Priors Cl GU14 13 G5
Priors Cl GU12 32 C3
Priors Keep GU52 23 F1
Priors La GU17 7 A6
Priory Cl GU51 22 B1
Priory Ct,
Camberley GU15 7 F6
Priory Ct,
Farnham GU9 34 D6
Priory St GU14 20 A3
Propeller Rd GU14 19 G5
Prospect Av GU14 19 G1
Prospect Rd,
Ash Vale GU12 27 E4
Prospect Rd,
Farnborough GU14 19 F3
Prospect Rd,
Rowledge GU10 36 B5
Providence Pl*,
Abbey St GU9 34 D4
Prunus Cl GU24 11 F5
Puckbridge Hill Rd
GU11 25 E4
Purley Way GU16 14 C5
Purmerend Cl GU14 18 B2
Pyestock Cres GU14 18 C3

Quarry Bank GU18 10 A3
Quarry La GU46 3 E3
Quebec Gdns GU17 12 D1
Queen Anne's Gate
GU9 30 D4
Queen Elizabeth Dr
GU11 31 F1
Queen Elizabeth Rd
GU15 8 A2
Queen Mary Av GU15 7 G6
Queen Mary Cl GU51 16 D4
Queen St GU12 32 B1
Queen Victoria Ct
GU14 19 H2
Queen Victorias Walk
GU15 7 E6
Queens Av GU11 25 G6
Queens Cl GU14 25 H2
Queens Cl GU14 26 A1
Queens Gate Rd GU14 25 G2
Queens La GU9 30 B5
Queens Mead GU15 7 F6
Queens Par Path GU11 25 H3
Queens Rd,
Aldershot GU11 31 E2
Queens Rd,
Camberley GU15 13 G1
Queens Rd,
Farnborough GU14 26 A1

Queens Rd,
Farnham GU9 30 B5
Queens Rd,
Fleet GU52 23 F2
Queensbury Pl GU17 12 C2
Queensmead GU14 19 H3
Queensway GU16 20 D1
Quennells Hill GU10 36 C2
Quetta Pk GU52 29 F1
Quinneys GU14 20 A6

Rackstraw Rd GU47 6 C2
Radcliffe Cl GU16 14 D6
Radford Cl GU9 30 D6
Rae Rd GU14 19 H6
Raeburn Way GU47 6 D5
Raf Gate Rd GU14 25 H1
Raglan Cl,
Aldershot GU12 31 H3
Raglan Cl,
Frimley Green GU16 14 D5
Ramilles Cl GU14 26 B2
Ramilles Pk GU11 26 B2
Ramilles Rd,
Aldershot GU12 26 A3
Ramilles Rd,
Aldershot GU11 26 A5
Ramsay Rd GU20 5 H3
Ramsdell Rd GU51 16 B4
Ramsey Cl GU15 9 E3
Randell Cl GU17 13 E4
Randolph Dr GU14 18 C4
Range Ride GU15 7 E4
Range Vw GU47 7 E3
Rapallo Cl GU14 19 H3
Rapley Cl GU15 8 C3
Rashleigh Ct GU52 23 F5
Rasset Mead GU52 22 C6
Ratcliffe Rd GU14 13 F5
Ravelin Cl GU16 28 B6
Raven Cl GU46 3 B3
Ravenscroft Cl GU14 27 F6
Ravenstone Rd GU15 9 G6
Ravenswood Dr GU15 8 C3
Rawdon Rise GU15 9 E6
Rawlinson Rd GU15 7 F5
Raygnoldes Ct GU52 22 C6
Reading Ct,
Blackwater GU17 12 B1
Reading Rd,
Farnborough GU14 19 H6
Reading Rd,
Yateley GU46 3 A1
Reading Rd North
GU13 16 B5
Reading Rd South
GU51,52 22 D1
Rebecca Cl GU52 22 C6
Recreation Rd GU10 36 B5
Rectory La GU20 5 F5
Rectory Rd GU14 19 H3
Red Lion La GU9 34 C4
Red Oaks GU10 36 A4
Red Rd GU18 9 G5
Redan Gdns GU12 31 H2
Redan Hill Est GU12 32 A2
Redan Rd GU12 31 H2
Redcrest Gdns GU15 8 C6
Rede Ct GU14 20 A6
Redfields La GU52 28 C2
Redlands La GU10 28 C4
Redmayne Cl GU15 15 F1
Redvers Buller Rd
GU11 26 A2
Redwood Dr GU15 15 G1
Redwoods Way GU52 23 F5
Reed Cl GU11 26 B4
Reeves Rd GU12 31 H2
Regent Cl GU51 23 F1
Regent Cl GU19 4 D6
Regent Ct*,
Albert St GU11 22 D1
Regent St GU51 23 F1
Regent Way GU14 14 D4
Regents Pl GU47 6 C3
Regiment Cl GU14 18 C4
Revelstoke Av GU14 19 G2
Revesby Cl GU14 11 E5
Reynolds Grn GU47 6 D5
Rhine Banks GU14 18 D2
Rhododendron Rd
GU16 14 D5
Ribble Pl GU14 19 E1
Richard Cl GU51 22 C2
Richards Cl GU12 27 E4
Richmond Cl,
Farnborough GU14 18 D4
Richmond Cl,
Fleet GU52 23 E3

Richmond Cl,
Frimley GU16 14 D4
Richmond Rd GU47 7 E3
Rideway Cl GU15 13 H1
Ridgemount Est GU16 15 F6
Ridgewood Dr GU15 15 G2
Ridgway Hill Rd GU9 34 D6
Ridgway Rd GU9 34 D6
Ridley Cl GU52 22 D2
Rifle Way GU14 18 C4
Rimbault Cl GU11 26 B2
Ringwood Cl,
Blackwater GU17 6 C5
Ringwood Rd,
Farnborough GU14 14 A6
Ripon Cl GU15 15 G2
Ripplesmore Cl GU47 6 B2
River La GU9 34 A6
River Rd GU46 3 B1
River Row GU9 34 A6
Riverdale GU10 36 B1
Rivermead Rd GU15 13 G3
Rivers Cl GU14 20 B6
Riverside Av GU18 10 D3
Riverside Bsns Pk
GU9 34 D2
Riverside Cl GU14 19 E3
Riverside Way GU15 13 F2
Robert Way GU16 20 C4
Roberts Rd GU12 32 A2
Robertson Way GU12 32 C2
Robin Cl GU12 26 D3
Robin Hill Dr GU15 14 D2
Robin Hood Cl GU14 13 F6
Robin La GU47 6 B3
Robins Bow GU15 13 H1
Robins Grove Cres
GU46 3 B2
Rochester Gro GU51 23 E1
Rock Gdns GU11 31 E2
Rock La GU10 36 D3
Rockfield Way GU47 6 D3
Rodmell Ct GU14 20 B6
Rokes Pl GU46 3 A3
Roman Way GU9 35 F1
Romayne Cl GU14 19 F2
Romley Ct GU9 34 D4
Romsey Cl,
Aldershot GU12 32 A5
Romsey Cl,
Blackwater GU17 6 C5
Rookwood Av GU47 6 D1
Rorkes Drift GU16 20 D3
Rosary Gdns GU46 3 D2
Rose Gdns GU14 18 D4
Rose Walk GU51 17 E5
Rosedale GU12 31 H2
Rosedene Gdns GU51 16 D5
Rosedene La GU47 6 D5
Rosemary Av GU12 26 D1
Rosemary Cl GU14 18 D3
Rosemary Gdns GU17 6 C6
Rosemary La,
Blackwater GU17 6 B6
Rosemary La,
Rowledge GU10 36 B4
Rosewood Way GU24 11 F5
Rosslea GU20 5 E2
Rosslyn Pl GU10 37 G2
Rossmore Gdns GU11 31 E3
Rothbury Walk GU15 15 F1
Rother Ct GU47 6 C3
Rother Rd GU14 19 E1
Rotherwick Ct GU14 25 H1
Rotherwick Ho GU51 16 B4
Rotten Green Rd RG27 16 C2
Rounce La GU24 11 E5
Round Cl GU46 3 F3
Roundway GU14 9 F5
Roundway Cl GU15 9 F5
Rounton Rd GU52 23 F4
Rowan Chase GU10 36 D2
Rowan Cl,
Camberley GU15 8 C3
Rowan Cl, Fleet GU51 23 G1
Rowan Dale GU52 22 D4
Rowans Cl GU14 13 E4
Rowcroft Cl GU12 26 D3
Rowhill Av GU11 31 F3
Rowhill Cres GU11 31 F3
Rowhills GU9 30 D3
Rowhills Cl GU9 31 E4
Roxbee Cox Rd GU14 17 H6
Roxburgh Cl GU15 15 F1
Royal Oak Cl GU46 3 E2
Royale Cl GU11 32 A4
Rubus Cl GU24 11 F5
Rudd Hall Rise GU15 14 B2
Rufford Cl GU52 23 E3

Rugby Cl GU47 — 7 E2
Rugosa Rd GU24 — 11 E5
Runford St George GU9
Runnymede Ct GU14 — 13 G6
Rushden Way GU9 — 30 C5
Rushmoor Cl GU52 — 23 E3
Rushmoor Ct GU14 — 25 H2
Rushmoor Rd GU11 — 24 D5
Russell Ct GU17 — 6 D6
Russet Cl GU10 — 32 C5
Russet Gdns GU15 — 7 H5
Russet Glade GU11 — 30 D3
Russetts Dr GU11 — 23 E4
Rustic Glen GU52 — 22 D4
Ruth Cl GU14 — 18 C2
Ryan Mt GU47 — 6 A3
Rydal Cl, Camberley GU15 — 9 G6
Rydal Cl, Farnborough GU14 — 18 D4
Rydal Dr GU52 — 22 D5
Rydal Pl GU18 — 10 B3
Ryde Gdns GU46 — 3 B2
Rye Cft GU52 — 22 D5
Rye Cl, Farnborough GU14 — 19 E1
Rye Cl, Fleet GU51 — 17 G2
Rye Gro GU24 — 11 F2
Ryebeck Rd GU52 — 23 E4
Ryecroft Gdns GU17 — 13 E1
Ryeland Cl GU51 — 17 G3
Ryelaw Rd GU52 — 23 E4
Ryle Rd GU9 — 34 C5
Ryves Av GU46 — 3 A3

Sabre Ct GU11 — 31 E2
Saddleback Rd GU15 — 8 B3
Saddleback Way GU51 — 17 F3
Saddler Cnr GU47 — 6 B4
Saddlewood GU15 — 13 H1
Saffron Ct GU14 — 18 C3
St Andrews Way GU14 — 14 C6
St Annes Glade GU19 — 4 B5
St Augustines Cl GU12 — 32 A2
St Benedicts Cl GU11 — 31 F3
St Catherines Rd GU16 — 14 D4
St Christophers Cl GU12 — 32 A1
St Christophers Pl GU14 — 19 F4
St Christophers Rd GU14 — 19 F4
St Clements Cl GU14 — 13 G6
St Cross Rd, Crondall GU10 — 28 B6
St Cross Rd, Farnham GU9 — 34 D2
St Cross Rd, Frimley Green GU16 — 15 E6
St Davids Cl, Farnborough GU14 — 13 E5
St Davids Cl, Farnham GU9 — 31 E5
St Georges Cl GU9 — 31 G6
St Georges Ct GU47 — 6 D1
St Georges Ind Est GU15 — 13 G2
St Georges Rd, Aldershot GU12 — 31 G3
St Georges Rd, Badshot Lea GU9 — 31 G6
St Georges Rd, Camberley GU15 — 8 A5
St Georges Rd, Farnham GU9 — 34 D4
St Georges Rd East GU12 — 31 H2
St Georges Yd GU9 — 34 C3
St Helens Cres GU47 — 6 B3
St James Av GU9 — 35 E2
St James Ct, Farnham GU9 — 34 D2
St James Ct, Fleet GU51 — 22 D1
St James Rd GU51 — 22 D1
St James Ter GU9 — 34 D2
St Johns Ct GU14 — 18 D3
St Johns Ct*, Clarence GU51 — 23 E1
St Johns Gro GU9 — 34 C6
St Johns Rd, Farnborough GU14 — 18 D3
St Johns Rd, Farnham GU9 — 34 C5
St Johns Rd, Sandhurst GU47 — 6 B4
St Josephs Rd GU12 — 31 G3

St Marks Cl GU14 — 20 A6
St Marks Pl GU9 — 30 B4
St Marys Cl GU47 — 6 C3
St Marys Gdns GU19 — 4 C5
St Marys Pl GU9 — 34 D2
St Marys Rd, Ash Vale GU12 — 26 D4
St Marys Rd, Camberley GU15 — 7 H5
St Michaels Cl GU51 — 23 G1
St Michaels Rd, Aldershot GU12 — 31 G3
St Michaels Rd, Camberley GU15 — 7 G1
St Michaels Rd, Farnborough GU14 — 19 H1
St Nicholas Cl GU51 — 16 D6
St Pauls Cl GU10 — 32 C5
St Peters Gdns, Wrecclesham GU10 — 36 C1
St Peters Gdns, Yateley GU46 — 3 B2
St Peters Mead GU12 — 33 E2
St Peters Pk GU11 — 31 E3
St Peters Way GU16 — 14 C6
St Philips Ct GU51 — 17 F6
Salamanca Pk GU14 — 31 F1
Salerno Cl GU11 — 31 F1
Salesian Vw GU14 — 26 B1
Salisbury Gro GU16 — 20 D4
Salisbury Rd, Ash GU12 — 33 E1
Salisbury Rd, Blackwater GU17 — 6 C6
Salisbury Rd, Farnborough GU14 — 19 H3
Salisbury Ter GU16 — 20 D5
Salmon Rd GU11 — 26 A4
Saltram Rd GU14 — 20 B5
Samarkand Cl GU15 — 15 E1
Sampson Bsns Pk GU15 — 13 G2
San Carlos App GU12 — 32 A1
Sand Hill GU14 — 13 G6
Sand Hill Ct GU14 — 13 G6
Sandford Cl GU11 — 31 E2
Sandford Rd, Aldershot GU11 — 31 E2
Sandford Rd, Farnham GU9 — 30 B4
Sandhurst La GU17 — 6 B5
Sandhurst Rd GU46 — 3 E2
Sandown Cl GU17 — 6 C6
Sandown Cres GU11 — 31 G4
Sandown Dr GU16 — 14 B3
Sandringham Ct GU14 — 25 H1
Sandringham Way GU16 — 14 C5
Sandrock Hill Rd GU10 — 36 C2
Sandy Hill Rd GU9 — 30 A4
Sandy La, Camberley GU15 — 8 B5
Sandy La, Church Crookham GU52 — 23 E5
Sandy La, Farnborough GU14 — 12 D6
Sandy La, Sandhurst GU47 — 6 B4
Sandy La, Tilford GU10 — 37 F6
Sankey La GU51 — 17 H3
Santina Cl GU14 — 30 C4
Sarah Way GU14 — 19 G3
Saunton Gdns GU14 — 19 F1
Saville Gdns GU15 — 9 E6
Savoy Gro GU17 — 12 D2
Saxon Cft GU9 — 34 D4
Saxony Way GU46 — 3 C4
Sayers Cl GU16 — 14 C6
Scarlet Oaks GU16 — 14 B2
Scarletts Rd GU11 — 25 G6
School Hill, Sandhurst GU47 — 6 A2
School Hill, Wrecclesham GU10 — 36 C1
School La, Bagshot GU19 — 4 B5
School La, Ewshot GU10 — 29 F3
School La, Lower Bourne GU10 — 37 G1
School La, Windlesham GU20 — 5 H3
School La, Yateley GU46 — 3 B3
School Rd, Rowledge GU10 — 36 B4

School Rd, Windlesham GU20 — 5 E2
Scotland Cl GU12 — 26 D4
Scotland Farm Rd GU12 — 26 D4
Scotland Hill GU47 — 6 A2
Scotts Ct GU14 — 13 G6
Scotts Grove Rd GU24 — 11 H5
Scutley La GU24 — 5 H6
Searle Rd GU15 — 34 D5
Seaton Rd GU15 — 7 H6
Sebastopol Rd GU11 — 31 G1
Sedgemoor GU14 — 13 H6
Seebys Oak GU47 — 6 D5
Sefton Cl GU24 — 11 G5
Selborne Av GU11 — 31 H5
Selborne Cl GU17 — 6 C5
Selborne Gdns GU9 — 34 B6
Selwyn Dr GU46 — 3 B2
Severn Cl GU47 — 6 C3
Severn Rd GU14 — 19 E1
Seymoor Ct GU51 — 17 E5
Seymour Dr GU15 — 9 E3
Shackleton Cl GU12 — 26 D4
Shady Nook GU9 — 30 B5
Shaftesbury Ct GU14 — 26 A1
Shaftesbury Mt GU17 — 12 C3
Shakespeare Gdns GU14 — 18 D2
Shalbourne Rise GU15 — 9 H3
Shalden Rd GU12 — 32 A3
Shaldon Way GU51 — 22 B1
Shamrock Cl GU16 — 14 B5
Shanklin Ct GU12 — 32 A2
Shawfield La GU12 — 32 C2
Shawfield Rd GU12 — 32 D6
Sheephouse GU9 — 34 D5
Sheffield Cl GU14 — 19 E3
Shelley Cl GU51 — 23 E1
Shelley Ct GU15 — 8 A6
Shelley Rise GU14 — 19 F2
Shelley Walk GU46 — 3 B4
Shepherds Chase GU19 — 4 C6
Shepherds Ct GU9 — 34 D5
Shepherds Walk GU14 — 12 D6
Sheraton Cl GU17 — 13 E1
Sherbourne Rd GU14 — 26 A1
Sheridan Cl GU11 — 31 C3
Sheridan Ct GU16 — 14 B5
Sheridan Rd GU16 — 14 A5
Sherington Cl GU14 — 19 G1
Sherwin Cres GU14 — 13 H6
Shetland Way GU51 — 17 F3
Shildon Cl GU15 — 15 G2
Ship Alley GU14 — 19 H1
Ship La GU14 — 20 A1
Shire Av GU51 — 17 G4
Shire Cl GU9 — 4 C6
Shire Ct GU11 — 31 E2
Shires Way GU46 — 3 D1
Shoe La GU11 — 25 F4
Short St GU11 — 31 F1
Shortdale Rd GU11 — 32 A5
Shortheath Crest GU9 — 36 C1
Shortheath Rd GU9 — 36 C1
Shrivenham Cl GU47 — 6 D3
Shrubbs La GU10 — 36 C4
Shrublands Dr GU15 — 10 B3
Sian Cl GU52 — 23 F4
Sidlaws Rd GU14 — 18 D1
Silchester Rd GU51 — 16 B4
Silver Birch Cl GU12 — 22 D5
Silver Dr GU16 — 15 F2
Silver Glades GU46 — 3 C4
Silver Hill GU47 — 7 E3
Silver Park Cl GU52 — 23 F3
Silverdale GU52 — 23 E3
Silverwood Dr GU15 — 8 D4
Silvester Way GU52 — 22 C5
Sine Cl GU14 — 13 G5
Sinhurst Rd GU15 — 13 G1
Slade La GU12 — 27 G6
Slim Cl GU11 — 26 B3
Slim Rd GU15 — 7 H4
Smithys Grn GU20 — 5 G4
Snailslynch GU9 — 35 E3
Snowdon Rd GU14 — 13 E6
Snowdrop Walk*, Stockton Pk GU15 — 17 E5
Snows Pad GU20 — 5 F1
Snows Ride GU20 — 5 F3
Solartron Rd GU14 — 19 G4
Somerset Rd GU14 — 26 A1
Somerville Cres GU46 — 3 E2
Sonninge Cl GU47 — 6 D3
Sorrel Cl GU14 — 18 C2
Sorrel Dr GU18 — 10 A4

South Atlantic Dr GU11 — 26 A6
South Av GU9 — 30 D5
South Farm La GU19 — 5 E6
South La GU12 — 33 E3
South Mall*, Upper St GU15 — 17 E6
South Side GU10 — 32 C5
South St, Ash Vale GU12 — 26 D5
South St, Farnborough GU14 — 20 B6
South St, Farnham GU9 — 34 D3
South Walk GU12 — 32 B1
Southampton Cl GU17 — 6 C5
Southampton St GU14 — 25 H1
Southby Dr GU51 — 8 D6
Southcote Dr GU15 — 7 H5
Southern Rd GU15 — 7 H5
Southern Way, Farnborough GU14 — 18 D5
Southern Way, Farnham GU9 — 34 D4
Southlands Cl GU12 — 33 E2
Southlands Rd GU12 — 33 E2
Southmead Rd GU11 — 31 G3
Southwark Cl GU46 — 3 C2
Southway GU15 — 13 G1
Southwell Park Rd GU15 — 7 H6
Southwick GU19 — 9 G2
Southwood Bsns Pk GU14
Southwood La GU14 — 18 C4
Southwood Rd GU14 — 18 D4
Sovereign Cl GU15 — 16 D6
Sovereign Dr GU15 — 9 E3
Sparrowhawk Cl GU10 — 29 F4
Sparvell Way GU15 — 8 A5
Spen Meade GU52 — 22 D6
Spencer Cl, Church Crookham GU52 — 23 G4
Spencer Cl, Frimley Green GU16 — 20 C2
Spoil La GU10 — 32 C4
Spokane Cl GU11 — 31 F3
Spring Gdns, Camberley GU15 — 9 E6
Spring Gdns, Farnborough GU14 — 19 H3
Spring La GU9 — 30 A5
Spring La West GU9 — 30 A5
Spring Woods, Fleet GU52 — 22 D3
Spring Woods, Sandhurst GU47 — 6 B2
Springcross Av GU17 — 12 D2
Springfield Gdns GU18 — 10 D3
Springfield La GU51 — 16 D6
Springfield Rd, Ash Vale GU12 — 26 D4
Springfield Rd, Camberley GU15 — 9 E6
Springholm Cl GU16 — 31 C6
Springlakes Ind Est GU12 — 26 B6
Springmead Ct GU47 — 7 E2
Spruce Dr GU18 — 10 B3
Spruce Way GU51 — 23 H1
Spurs Ct GU11 — 31 E2
Squirrel Cl GU47 — 6 B3
Squirrel La GU14 — 19 F2
Stable Cft GU19 — 4 B6
Stable Vw GU46 — 3 D1
Staff College Rd GU15 — 7 F5
Staff Rd GU12 — 32 A2
Stake La GU14 — 19 F3
Stamford Av GU16 — 14 C4
Stanhope Rd GU15 — 7 F6
Stanley Dr GU14 — 18 C4
Stanton Dr GU51 — 22 D1
Star La GU12 — 32 D2
Star Post Rd GU15 — 8 C3
Station App, Ash Vale GU12 — 26 D2
Station App, Blackwater GU17 — 13 E1
Station App, Farnborough GU14 — 19 H3
Station App, Fleet GU51 — 17 F4
Station App, Frimley GU16 — 14 A5
Station Hill GU9 — 34 D4
Station Rd, Aldershot GU11 — 31 G2

Station Rd, Bagshot GU19 — 4
Station Rd, Farnborough GU14 — 19
Station Rd, Frimley GU16 — 14
Station Rd East GU12 — 26
Station Rd West GU12 — 26
Station Vw GU12 — 26
Steeles Rd GU11 — 15
Steerforth Copse GU47 — 7
Stephendale Rd GU9 — 35
Stevens Hill GU46 — 3
Stewards Rise*, Keable Rd GU9 — 36
Stilwell Cl GU46 — 3
Stirling Cl, Ash Vale GU12 — 26
Stirling Cl, Farnborough GU14 — 19
Stirling Cl, Frimley GU16 — 14
Stirling Gdns GU47 — 6
Stockbridge Dr GU11 — 32
Stockbridge Way GU14 — 32
Stockton Av GU51 — 17
Stockton Pk GU51 — 17
Stockwood Rise GU15 — 8
Stockwood Way GU9 — 3
Stoke Hills GU9 — 34
Stone St GU12 — 32
Stonegate GU15 — 9
Stonehill Rd GU18 — 10
Stonehouse Rise GU16 — 14
Stoneleigh Ct GU14 — 14
Stoney Cl GU46 — 3
Stoneyfields GU9 — 35
Stookes Way GU46 — 3
Stourhead Cl GU14 — 20
Stovolds Way GU11 — 3
Stratford Ct, Farnborough GU14 — 19
Stratford Ct, Farnham GU9 — 34
Stratford Rd GU12 — 26
Strathmore Ct GU15 — 8
Stratton Walk GU14 — 13
Stream Farm Cl GU10 — 37
Stream Valley Rd GU10 — 3
Streamside GU51 — 23
Street End RG27 — 23
Streets Heath GU24 — 11
Stroud La GU51 — 22
Stuart Cl GU14 — 19
Stubbs Folly GU47 — 6
Stubbs Ind Site GU11
Stubbs Moor Rd GU14 — 19
Sturdee Cl GU16 — 14
Sturt Rd, Farnham GU9 — 30
Sturt Rd, Frimley Green GU16
Suffolk Cl GU19 — 4
Sullivan Cl GU14 — 19
Sullivan Rd GU15 — 19
Summer Gdns GU15 — 9
Summerfield La GU10 — 36
Summit Av GU14 — 18
Sumner Cl GU9 — 34
Sumner Rd GU9 — 34
Sun Ray Est GU47 — 6
Sundew Cl GU18 — 10
Sunninghill Rd GU20 — 5
Sunny Hill Rd GU11 — 30
Sunnybank Mws GU12 — 2
Sunnybank Rd GU14 — 2
Sunnydell La GU10 — 36
Sunnyside GU51 — 16
Surbiton Rd GU15 — 8
Surrey Av GU15 — 13
Surridge Ct GU19 — 9
Sussex Gdns GU15 — 8
Sutton Rd GU15 — 8
Swale Rd GU14 — 19
Swaledale Gdns GU51 — 17
Swallow Cl GU10 — 36
Swan La GU47 — 6
Swan Way GU51 — 22
Swift La GU19 — 4
Swift Rd GU9 — 30
Swifts Cl GU10 — 35
Swingate Rd GU9 — 34
Swinley Rd GU20 — 4
Swiss Cl GU10 — 36
Switchback La GU10 — 36

amore Cl,
  nley GU16 14 B4
amore Cl,
  ndhurst GU47 6 B3
amore Cres GU51 22 C3
amore Dr,
  n Vale GU12 26 D2
amore Dr,
  nley GU16 14 B3
amore Dr,
  ecclesham GU10 36 D2
amore Rd GU14 20 A5
hey Villas GU12 26 D2
an Ridge GU47 6 A2
an Way GU52 22 D4
n Pl GU14 20 B4

ey Cl GU51 16 C4
ole La GU10 29 F2
vera Pk GU11 31 G1
ot Cl GU16 20 D3
ot Pl GU19 4 C4
ot Rd GU9 34 C5
arth Dr GU14 20 B5
worth Dr GU51 17 F3
ier Ct GU11 31 E2
lewood Ride
  24 11 E4
  Rd GU47 7 E6
er Rd GU14 19 H6
ers Yd GU19 4 B5
at Ct GU47 6 D3
Cl GU14 18 D5
gon Cl GU14 18 B3
stock Gdns GU14 19 G1
stock Rd GU13 16 B6
t GU14 19 E1
ls Av GU15 8 A6
ls Ct GU15 14 B1
ls Way GU15 14 C2
olar Av GU14 19 F6
olar Cl GU47 6 A3
Acre Walk GU10 36 C4
y Rd GU16 14 D5
Cotta Cl GU10 36 C2
mond Dr GU46 3 A3
nes Cl GU14 19 E1
Alders GU9 31 C6
Aloes GU51 23 F1
Arcade GU11 31 G1
Ashtrees GU12 33 F1
Avenue,
  ershot GU12 32 A4
Avenue,
  nberley GU15 7 H5
Avenue,
  et GU51 16 C6
ntwater GU18 10 A2
Avenue,
  vledge GU10 36 B4
Beck Ind Est
  12 32 B3
Beeches GU12 26 D1
Birches,
  ckwater GU17 6 B6
Birches,
  nborough GU14 18 D3
Borough,
  ndall GU10 28 B5
Borough,
  ham GU9 34 C3
Bourne GU52 23 E3
Bowlings GU15 8 A5
Breech GU47 7 E4
Briars, Ash GU12 33 E2
Briars,
  rch Crookham
  52 23 F4
Broadway GU47 6 B4
Brook Trading Est
  12 32 B1
Buchan GU12 8 D3
Buntings GU9 34 A6
Byfrons GU9 20 A5
Cedars GU51 23 F1
Chantrys GU9 34 A4
Chase GU14 20 A2
Chine GU10 36 C2
Cloisters GU16 14 B4
Close,
  ege Town GU47 7 E3
Close,
  ham GU9 35 E5
  ley GU16 14 A5
Close,
  twater GU18 10 B2

The Copse,
  Farnborough GU14 18 D5
The Copse,
  Rowledge GU10 36 C4
The Covert GU14 13 E5
The Crescent,
  Blackwater GU17 12 D1
The Crescent,
  Crookham Village
  GU51 22 A3
The Crescent,
  Farnborough GU14 19 H4
The Crescent,
  Farnham GU9 30 C4
The Crescent,
  Yateley GU46 3 D2
The Croft, Fleet GU51 22 B1
The Croft,
  Yateley GU46 3 D2
The Dell GU46 3 C3
The Drive GU9 34 C6
The Elms,
  Blackwater GU17 12 D1
The Elms,
  Tongham GU10 32 C4
The Fairfield GU9 34 D4
The Fairway,
  Farnborough GU14 18 A6
The Fairway,
  Farnham GU9 30 D4
The Fairway,
  Frimley GU16 14 D2
The Ferns GU9 30 C4
The Findings GU14 13 E5
The Flats GU17 12 B1
The Gallop GU46 3 D1
The Gardens GU10 32 C4
The Garth, Ash GU12 32 C3
The Garth,
  Farnborough GU14 20 A3
The Gates GU51 17 G3
The Glade GU9 30 D4
The Glebe GU17 13 E1
The Glen GU9 30 C5
The Green,
  Badshot Lea GU9 31 G6
The Green,
  Blackwater GU17 6 B6
The Green,
  Farnham GU9 30 C5
The Green,
  Frimley Green GU16 20 C1
The Grove,
  Aldershot GU11 31 G2
The Grove,
  Farnborough GU14 20 A6
The Grove,
  Frimley GU16 14 B4
The Hart GU9 34 C3
The Hatches,
  Farnham GU9 34 A6
The Hatches,
  Frimley Green GU16 20 C1
The Heights GU15 8 B6
The Howf GU14 18 B6
The Jollies GU10 28 B5
The Laburnums GU17 6 B6
The Lake Side GU17 12 D1
The Laurels,
  Farnham GU9 31 E4
The Laurels,
  Fleet GU51 17 E6
The Lawns GU14 18 D4
The Lea GU51 22 C2
The Lindens GU9 35 E5
The Link GU46 3 C2
The Long Rd GU10 36 C5
The Mallards GU16 14 C3
The Maultway GU15 9 E3
The Mead GU14 19 H4
The Meadows GU12 33 F1
The Meadows Retail Pk
  GU47 7 E6
The Moors GU10 32 C4
The Mount GU51 17 E5
The Mulberries GU9 35 G1
The Oaks,
  Farnborough GU14 18 D4
The Oaks, Fleet GU13 16 B6
The Oaks,
  Yateley GU46 3 D4
The Old Orch GU9 34 B6
The Orchard GU18 10 B3
The Paddock GU10 36 C3
The Parade, Ash GU12 26 D5
The Parade,
  Frimley GU16 14 A5
The Parade,
  Yateley GU46 3 E2

The Pathfinders GU14 18 C4
The Pavilions End
  GU15 14 B2
The Pines GU15 8 C4
The Potteries GU14 18 C1
The Quadrant GU12 26 D5
The Reeds Rd GU10 37 G6
The Ridgeway GU18 10 B2
The Ridings GU16 15 E2
The Rockery GU14 18 D4
The Romany GU14 18 A6
The Royal Way GU16 15 G5
The Sett GU46 3 B3
The Shrubbery GU14 18 D4
The Sidings GU11 31 H1
The Southwood Cres
  GU14 18 D4
The Spinney,
  Camberley GU15 9 F5
The Spinney,
  Fleet GU51 22 C1
The Spinney,
  Yateley GU46 3 C2
The Square,
  Bagshot GU19 4 C5
The Square,
  Lightwater GU18 10 C2
The Street,
  Crookham Village
  GU51 22 B4
The Street,
  Tongham GU10 32 C6
The Street,
  Wrecclesham GU10 36 C1
The Sycamores,
  Blackwater GU17 6 B6
The Sycamores,
  Farnborough GU14 20 A4
The Terrace GU15 7 F6
The Topiary GU14 19 E5
The Verne GU52 23 E4
The Warren,
  Aldershot GU11 31 F2
The Warren,
  Farnham GU9 30 D4
The Wellington Centre*,
  Little Wellington St
  GU11 31 G1
The Willows GU18 10 D2
The Withes GU10 28 B5
The Woodbarn*,
  Wessex Pl GU9 34 D4
The Wrekin GU14 20 B6
Theal Ct GU47 6 D3
Theobalds Way GU16 15 F2
Thibet Rd GU47 6 C3
Thirlmere Cl GU14 19 E4
Thirlmere Cres GU52 22 D5
Thirlmere Walk GU15 15 G1
Thirsk Ct GU12 32 A1
Thorburn Chase GU47 6 D5
Thorn Cl GU14 20 A4
Thorn Rd GU10 36 D3
Thorndown La GU20 5 G5
Thornfield Grn GU17 13 E2
Thornhill Rd GU11 26 A5
Thornyhurst Rd GU16 20 D3
Thorold Rd GU9 34 D2
Three Stiles Rd GU9 34 A3
Threshers Cnr GU15 17 G3
Throgmorton Rd GU46 3 A3
Thurbans Rd GU9 36 D1
Thyme Ct GU14 18 C2
Tichborne Cl GU17 6 D6
Tichborne Pl GU12 32 A4
Tichbourne Cl GU14 14 C2
Tile Barn Cl GU14 19 G2
Tilford Rd GU9 34 D4
Timber Bank GU16 20 D2
Timber Cl*,
  The Hart GU9 34 C3
Tindal Cl GU46 3 D2
Tintagel Dr GU16 14 C4
Tiverton Way GU14 18 D4
Toad La GU17 13 E1
Tockington Ct GU46 3 D2
Tolpuddle Way GU46 3 F3
Tomlins Av GU16 14 C3
Tomlinscote Way
  GU16 14 D3
Tongham Rd,
  Aldershot GU11 32 A4
Tongham Rd,
  Farnham GU9 32 A6
Toplady Pl GU10 36 D3
Tor Rd GU9 34 A3
Totland Ct GU14 19 G1
Tottenham Walk GU47 6 D2
Toulouse Cl GU15 9 E4

Tournai Cl GU11 26 B3
Tower Hill GU14 19 F4
Town Sq GU15 8 A5
Townside Pl GU15 8 A5
Trafalgar Ct GU9 34 C4
Trafalgar Way GU15 13 F1
Trafford Rd GU16 14 A5
Transport Rd GU14 19 H6
Travis La GU47 6 C4
Trebor Av GU9 34 D5
Tredenham Cl GU14 25 H1
Tree Tops Av GU15 9 E3
Treeside Dr GU14 31 E4
Tregolls Dr GU14 20 A4
Tremayne Walk GU15 15 F1
Trent Cl GU14 19 E1
Trenton Cl GU16 14 D4
Trimmers Cl GU9 30 B4
Trinity GU47 7 E1
Trinity Flds GU9 30 A5
Trinity Hill GU9 30 A5
Trotwood Cl GU47 7 E1
Troutbeck Walk GU15 15 G2
Trunk Rd GU14 18 B3
Tryplets GU52 22 C6
Tudor Cl GU12 32 C2
Tudor Dr GU46 3 D4
Tudor Way GU52 23 F5
Tumber Ct GU12 32 D2
Tunworth Cl GU51 16 C3
Turf Hill Rd GU15 8 C3
Turner Pl GU47 6 D5
Turners Av GU51 16 C4
Turners Green La,
  Hook RG27 16 A3
Turners Green La,
  Hook RG27 16 C2
Turners Way GU51 16 C4
Turnstone End GU46 3 B3
Turnville Cl GU18 10 B2
Turpins Rise GU20 5 E2
Tuscam Way GU15 13 F1
Tweed Cl GU14 19 E1
Tweedsmuir Cl GU14 18 C4
Twelve Acre Cres
  GU14 18 D2
Tweseldown Rd GU52 23 F5
Twisell Thorne GU52 22 D5
Twyford La GU10 37 E2
Tyne Cl GU14 19 E1

Ullswater Av GU14 18 D4
Ullswater Cl,
  Farnham GU9 30 A5
Ullswater Cl,
  Lightwater GU18 10 C2
Ullswater Ct*,
  Lakeside Cl GU12 26 C5
Ullswater Rd GU18 10 C2
Underhill La GU10 37 E1
Underwood Av GU12 32 C3
Union Cl GU47 6 D1
Union Rd,
  Blackdown Barracks
  GU16 15 G5
Union Rd,
  Farnham GU9 34 D4
Union St,
  Aldershot GU11 31 G1
Union St,
  Farnborough GU14 19 G3
Union Ter GU11 31 G1
Updown Hill GU20 5 G4
Upland Rd GU15 8 A4
Uplands Cl GU47 6 B3
Uplands Rd GU9 35 F4
Upper Bourne La
  GU10 36 D3
Upper Bourne Vale
  GU10 36 D2
Upper Charles St GU15 7 H5
Upper Chobham Rd
  GU16 14 D2
Upper Church La GU34 3 C3
Upper College Ride
  GU15 8 B4
Upper Elms Rd GU11 31 F2
Upper Froyle Dr GU51 16 C4
Upper Gordon Rd
  GU15 8 A6
Upper Hale Rd GU9 30 A5
Upper Mount St GU51 16 B4
Upper Old Park La
  GU9 30 A6
Upper Park Rd GU15 8 A6
Upper Pinewood Rd
  GU12 27 G6
Upper St Michaels Rd
  GU11 31 G3

Upper South Vw GU9 34 D2
Upper St, Fleet GU51 22 D1
Upper St, Fleet GU51 23 E1
Upper Union St*,
  Barrack Rd GU11 31 F1
Upper Union Ter*,
  Cross St GU14 31 G1
Upper Verran Rd
  GU15 14 A2
Upper Way GU9 34 B6
Upper Weybourne La
  GU9 30 D4
Upton Cl GU14 20 B4
Upton Grey Dr GU51 16 C4

Vale Cl GU10 37 F3
Vale Rd,
  Ash Vale GU12 26 D3
Vale Rd,
  Camberley GU15 13 G1
Vale Wood Dr GU10 37 F3
Valley La GU10 37 F3
Valley Rd GU16 15 E5
Valley Vw GU47 6 A4
Valroy Cl GU15 8 A5
Varney Cl GU14 19 E2
Velmead Cl GU52 23 F2
Velmead Rd GU52 23 E2
Ventnor Ter GU12 31 H2
Verge Walk GU11 31 G4
Vernon Ct GU9 34 B4
Veronica Dr GU51 22 B4
Verran Rd GU15 14 A2
Vesey Cl GU14 19 G2
Viburnum Ct GU24 11 F5
Vicarage Cl GU9 35 E6
Vicarage Gdns GU52 23 E5
Vicarage Hill GU52 35 E6
Vicarage La,
  Farnham GU9 34 C4
Vicarage La,
  The Bourne GU9 35 E6
Vicarage La,
  Upper Hale GU9 30 C4
Vicarage La,
  Yateley GU46 3 C1
Vicarage Rd,
  Blackwater GU17 13 E1
Vicarage Rd,
  Yateley GU46 3 B1
Vickers Rd GU12 26 C4
Victoria Av GU15 7 G6
Victoria Ct,
  Bagshot GU19 9 H2
Victoria Ct, Fleet GU51 17 E6
Victoria Dr GU17 12 C1
Victoria Gdns GU51 16 D6
Victoria Hill Rd GU51 16 C6
Victoria Rd,
  Aldershot GU11 31 G2
Victoria Rd,
  Farnborough GU14 19 G3
Victoria Rd,
  Farnham GU9 34 D3
Victoria Rd,
  Fleet GU51 16 D6
Victoria Rd,
  Owlsmoor GU47 6 D2
Vienna Ct GU14 19 G1
Vigo La GU46 3 C4
Village Way GU46 3 D2
Vine Cl,
  Aldershot GU11 25 G3
Vine Cl,
  Wrecclesham GU10 36 D3
Vine House Cl GU16 20 D4
Vine La GU10 36 D3
Vine St GU11 31 F2
Vine Way GU10 36 D3
Virginia Gdns GU14 20 A5
Viscount Cl GU12 26 D4
Vivian Cl GU52 23 F3
Vulcan Cl GU47 6 A4
Vulcan Ct GU47 6 A4
Vulcan Way GU47 6 A4

Wadham GU47 7 E2
Waggoners Hollow
  GU19 4 C6
Wakefords Pk GU14 23 F6
Waldorf Heights GU17 12 D2
Walkers Ridge GU15 9 E4
Wallace Way GU11 31 E1
Wallington Rd GU15 8 D2
Walmer Cl GU16 14 D6
Walnut Cl,
  Aldershot GU11 31 G4
Walnut Cl,
  Yateley GU46 3 D4

Waltham Cl GU47 6 D2
Walton Cl GU51 22 D1
Wandle Cl GU12 33 E2
Wandsdyke Cl GU16 14 C5
Wantage Rd GU47 6 D3
Wardle Cl GU19 4 C5
Wargrove Dr GU47 6 D3
Warren Cl, Fleet GU51 23 F2
Warren Cl,
  Sandhurst GU47 6 A3
Warren Cnr GU10 29 E4
Warren Rise GU16 14 D2
Warrington Mws GU11 31 E3
Warwick Cl,
  Aldershot GU11 31 H3
Warwick Cl,
  Camberley GU15 15 E2
Warwick Rd GU12 26 D1
Wasdale Cl GU47 6 D1
Watchetts Dr GU15 13 H3
Watchetts Lake Cl
  GU15 14 A2
Watchetts Rd GU15 13 H2
Watchmoor Pk GU15 13 G1
Watchmoor Rd GU15 13 G1
Watchmoor Trading Est
  GU15 13 G2
Water La,
  Farnborough GU14 13 F6
Water La,
  Farnham GU9 35 F1
Water Rede GU52 22 D6
Waterfront Bsns Pk
  GU51 17 F4
Waterhouse Mead
  GU47 6 D4
Waterloo Cl GU15 9 E4
Waterloo Rd GU12 31 H2
Waterside Ct GU51 17 F4
Waterside Mws GU51 17 F4
Watery La GU52 22 C6
Watts Rd GU14 19 F2
Waverley Av GU51 17 E5
Waverley Cl GU15 14 D1
Waverley Cl*,
  Waverley La GU9 35 E4
Waverley Dr GU12 26 D4
Waverley Gdns GU12 26 D4
Waverley La GU9 35 E4
Waverley Rd,
  Bagshot GU19 4 C5
Waverley Rd,
  Camberley GU15 8 C6
Waverley Rd,
  Farnborough GU14 20 A4
Wayman Rd GU14 12 D5
Waynflete La GU9 34 A4
Ways End GU15 14 B1
Weapon Rd GU14 19 G5
Weaver Moss GU47 6 B4
Weavers Gdns GU9 36 C1
Webb Cl GU19 9 H1
Weir Av GU14 19 F4
Weir Cl GU14 19 F4
Weir Rd GU14 18 A5
Welbeck Cl GU14 18 A5
Weldon Cl GU52 23 F4
Well Cl GU15 13 H1
Well Rd GU10 28 A6
Wellburn Cl GU47 6 B4
Weller Dr GU15 13 H2
Wellesley Cl,
  Ash Vale GU12 26 C2
Wellesley Cl,
  Bagshot GU19 4 A5
Wellesley Gate GU12 31 G2
Wellesley Gdns GU9 30 B5
Wellesley Rd GU11 30 D1
Wellington Av,
  Aldershot GU11 31 E1
Wellington Av,
  Fleet GU51 17 F5
Wellington Cl GU47 6 C3
Wellington Gdns GU11 31 F2
Wellington La GU9 30 D4
Wellington Pl GU12 26 C5
Wellington Rd GU47 6 B3
Wellington St GU11 31 G1
Wellington Ter GU47 6 C3
Wellingtonia Av GU15 9 G6
Wells Cotts GU9 36 D1

Wendover Dr GU16 15 F2
Wensley Dr GU51 17 E4
Wensleydale Dr GU15 9 G6
Wentworth Cl,
  Ash Vale GU12 26 D3
Wentworth Cl,
  Farnham GU9 31 E5
Wentworth Cl,
  Yateley GU46 3 D3
Wentworth Cres GU12 26 D3
Wessex Pl GU9 34 D4
West Av GU9 30 D5
West Cl GU9 30 D5
West End Gro GU9 34 B4
West Fryerne GU46 3 D1
West Glade GU14 18 D3
West Grn GU46 3 B2
West Heath Rd GU14 19 E3
West Rd,
  Camberley GU15 8 B6
West Rd,
  Farnborough GU14 13 G6
West Ring GU10 32 D4
West St GU9 34 A5
West Station Rd GU11 31 G2
West Tisted Cl GU51 16 C4
Westbourne Rd GU47 7 E4
Westbury Cl GU51 23 H1
Westbury Gdns,
  Farnham GU9 35 E1
Westbury Gdns,
  Fleet GU51 23 H1
Westbury Way GU12 32 A1
Westerdale Dr GU16 15 E2
Western Rd GU11 31 E2
Westfield Ct*,
  Clarence Rd GU51 17 E6
Westfield La GU10 36 B1
Westfield Rd GU15 13 H3
Westmead GU14 19 G4
Westminster Cl GU51 17 E5
Westmorland Dr GU16 15 E2
Weston Gro GU19 4 D4
Westover Rd GU51 17 F6
Westwood Rd GU20 5 G3
Wetherby Gdns GU14 26 A1
Wey Cl, Ash GU12 32 D2
Wey Cl,
  Camberley GU15 7 G6
Weybank Cl GU9 34 D3
Weybourne Rd GU9 31 E5
Weybridge Mead
  GU46 3 E2
Weydon Hill Cl GU9 34 C5
Weydon Hill Rd GU9 34 C5
Weydon La GU9 34 A6
Weydon Mill La GU9 34 B5
Weyside GU9 34 D4
Weywood Cl GU9 31 F5
Weywood La GU9 31 F5
Wharf Rd, Ash GU12 27 E5
Wharf Rd,
  Frimley Green GU16 20 C1
Wharf Way GU16 20 D1
Wharfenden Way
  GU16 20 D1
Wheatley Rd GU11 31 F1
Whetstone Rd GU14 18 C3
Whin Holt GU52 23 E3
Whins Cl GU15 13 H1
Whins Dr GU15 13 H1
Whistler Gro GU47 6 D5
Whitby Cl GU14 20 B6
Whitchurch Cl GU11 32 A5
Whitchurch Rd GU51 16 C4
White Acres Rd GU16 20 C3
White Cottage Cl GU9 30 D6
White Hart Ind Est
  GU17 7 E6
White Hart Par GU17 13 E1
White Hill GU20 5 F2
White House Gdns
  GU46 3 D2
White House Walk
  GU9 30 D4
White La GU10,12 33 F3
White Lion Way GU46 3 D2
White Post La GU10 36 D3
White Rd GU15 7 E5
White Rose La GU10 34 E1

Whitebeam Gdns
  GU14 18 C4
Whitehill Cl GU15 8 A4
Whitehouse Cl GU14 19 G1
Whites Rd GU14 20 B6
Whitethorn Cl GU12 33 E3
Whitlet Cl GU9 34 C4
Whitley Rd GU46 3 D4
Whitmoor Rd GU19 4 D5
Whitmore Cl GU47 6 D3
Whitmore Grn GU9 30 D6
Whittle Cl,
  Aldershot GU12 26 C4
Whittle Cl,
  Sandhurst GU47 6 A2
Whittle Cres GU14 19 E1
Whyte Av GU12 32 A4
Wicket Hill GU10 36 D2
Wickham Cl,
  Bagshot GU19 4 C2
Wickham Cl,
  Church Crookham
  GU52 22 D4
Wickham Ct GU51 22 C3
Wickham Pl GU52 22 D3
Wickham Rd,
  Camberley GU15 8 C3
Wickham Rd,
  Church Crookham
  GU52 22 D4
Wilderness Rd GU16 14 C3
Wilders Cl GU16 14 B2
Wildwood Gdns GU46 3 C4
Willems Av GU11 31 E1
William Farthing Cl
  GU11 31 E1
Williams Way GU51 17 G6
Willington Cl GU15 7 H5
Willow Cl GU16 20 C3
Willow Cres GU14 13 G6
Willow Ct,
  Ash Vale GU12 26 D2
Willow Ct,
  Frimley GU16 14 B4
Willow Grn GU24 11 G5
Willow La GU17 12 D1
Willow Pk GU12 32 C1
Willow Way,
  Aldershot GU12 32 B3
Willow Way,
  Farnham GU9 30 D5
Willowford GU46 3 D2
Willows End GU47 6 B3
Wilmot Way GU15 14 C2
Wilson Rd,
  Aldershot GU12 32 A3
Wilson Rd,
  Farnborough GU14 19 F4
Wilton Ct GU14 20 B4
Wilton Rd GU15 13 H2
Wimbledon Cl GU15 8 C2
Wimbledon Rd GU15 8 C2
Winchcombe Cl GU51 23 E1
Winchester Rd GU12 26 D6
Winchester St GU14 25 F1
Winchester Way GU17 6 C5
Winchfield Cl GU51 16 C4
Windermere Cl GU14 18 D4
Windermere Ct*,
  Lakeside Cl GU12 26 C5
Windermere Rd GU18 10 C2
Windermere Walk
  GU15 13 H1
Windermere Way GU9 30 A5
Winding Wood Rd
  GU16 15 E2
Windle Cl GU20 5 H4
Windlesham Ct GU20 5 G1
Windlesham Rd GU24 11 F3
Windmill Fld GU20 5 G4
Windmill Rd GU12 31 H2
Windrush Heights
  GU47 6 A3
Windsor Cl GU14 19 G4
Windsor Cres GU9 30 B6
Windsor Ct GU51 17 H6
Windsor Gdns GU12 32 C2
Windsor Rd GU14 20 A6
Windsor Ride GU15 7 G4
Windsor Way,
  Aldershot GU11 31 G2

Windsor Way,
  Frimley Green GU16 14 C5
Wingate Ct GU11 31 F1
Wingfield Gdns GU16 15 G2
Wings Rd GU9 30 B5
Winkworth Pl*,
  St James Ter GU9 34 D2
Winston Cl GU16 20 C1
Winston Walk GU10 37 E1
Winterbourne Walk
  GU16 14 C5
Winton Cres GU46 3 D3
Winton Rd,
  Aldershot GU11 31 F3
Winton Rd,
  Farnham GU9 35 E2
Wishmoor Cl GU15 8 B3
Wishmoor Rd GU15 8 C3
Wisley Gdns GU14 18 D5
Wistaria La GU46 3 C3
Withy Cl GU18 10 D2
Wittmead Rd GU16 20 D3
Woburn Av GU14 20 B3
Woburn Cl GU16 14 D4
Wolfe Rd GU12 32 A2
Wolseley Rd GU11 31 G2
Wood La,
  Farnborough GU14 19 F4
Wood La, Fleet GU51 17 G6
Wood Rd,
  Farnham GU9 30 C5
Wood Rd,
  Frimley GU15 13 H4
Wood St GU12 26 D4
Woodbine Cl GU47 6 B4
Woodbourne GU9 31 E4
Woodbourne Cl GU46 3 D3
Woodbridge Dr GU15 8 B4
Woodbridge Rd GU17 6 B6
Woodcot Gdns GU14 18 D3
Woodcote Grn GU51 22 B1
Woodcott Ter GU12 32 A3
Woodcut Rd GU10 36 C2
Woodend GU14 20 A4
Woodend Rd GU16 15 F6
Woodgate GU51 17 G4
Woodland Ct*,
  Annettes Cft GU52 22 D5
Woodland Dr GU10 37 E1
Woodland Rise GU22 20 A4
Woodlands GU51 17 E5
Woodlands Av GU9 31 E4
Woodlands Cl,
  Ash GU12 27 E5
Woodlands Cl,
  Blackwater GU17 13 E4
Woodlands Ct GU47 7 E2
Woodlands La GU20 5 H4
Woodlands Rd,
  Camberley GU15 7 G6
Woodlands Rd,
  Farnborough GU14 18 D1
Woodlands Walk GU14 12 D4
Woodleigh GU51 23 E1
Woodpecker Cl GU10 29 F4
Woodside,
  Blackwater GU17 12 C3
Woodside,
  Farnborough GU14 13 H6
Woodside Gdns GU51 17 G6
Woodside Rd,
  Farnborough GU14 25 F2
Woodside Rd,
  Farnham GU9 31 E4
Woodstocks GU14 20 A2
Woodville Cl GU17 6 B6
Woodway GU15 7 G6
Woollards Rd GU12 27 E5
Woolmead Rd GU9 34 D3
Woolmead Walk*,
  Woolmead Rd GU9 34 D3
Worcester Cl GU14 13 H6
Wordsworth Av GU46 3 B3
Worsley Rd GU16 14 C6
Wrecclesham Hill
  GU10 36 A4
Wrecclesham Rd GU9 34 A6
Wren Cl GU46 3 B2
Wren Ct GU12 33 E1
Wren Way GU14 13 F6
Wychelm Rd GU18 10 D3

Wychwood Cl GU12 32
Wychwood Pl GU15 32
Wyke Av GU12 33
Wyke Bungalows
  GU12 33
Wyke La GU12 33
Wykeham Rd GU9 34
Wymering Ct GU14 20
Wyndham Cl GU46 2
Wyndham St GU12 3
Wynfields GU16 2
Wynne Gdns GU52 2
Wynsham Way GU20 2
Wyvern Cl GU14 2

Yale Cl GU47
Yateley Rd GU47
Yatesbury Cl GU9 3
Yaverland Dr GU19
Yeomans Cl,
  Farnborough GU14 1
Yeomans Cl,
  Tongham GU10 3
Yeomans Way GU15
Yeovil Cl GU14 2
Yeovil Rd,
  Farnborough GU14 2
Yeovil Rd,
  Owlsmoor GU47
Yetminster Rd GU14 2
Yew Tree Cl GU14 1
Yew Tree Walk GU16 1
Yockley Cl GU15 1
Yolland Cl GU9 3
York Cres GU11 3
York Pl GU15
York Rd,
  Aldershot GU11 3
York Rd, Ash GU12 3
York Rd,
  Camberley GU15
York Rd,
  Farnborough GU14 2
York Rd,
  Farnham GU9 3
York Rd,
  North Camp GU14 2
York Town Ind Est
  GU15 1
York Way GU47
Yorktown Rd GU47
Youlden Cl GU15
Youlden Dr GU15
Youngs Dr GU12 3

Zenith Ct GU47